A NARRATIVE OF THE LATE TRANSACTIONS AT BENARES

A
NARRATIVE OF THE LATE TRANSACTIONS AT BENARES

WARREN HASTINGS, Esq.

GYAN

Published by

GYAN

Gyan Publishing House
5, Ansari Road
Daryaganj, New Delhi-110002
Phone: 011-47034999, 9811692060
E-mail: books@gyanbooks.com

Distribution Network
gyanbooks.com
India, USA, Canada, UK, Australia, France

ISBN : 978-81-212-9640-3 (PB)
First Published, 1782

2nd Impression 2023

Printed at: Gyan Press, Delhi.

A NARRATIVE OF THE LATE TRANSACTIONS AT BENARES
Author: WARREN HASTINGS

A NARRATIVE

OF THE LATE TRANSACTIONS AT BENARES.

By WARREN HASTINGS, Esq.

1782.

TO

Edward Wheler, Esq.

&c. &c. &c. and Council.

Fort William.

Gentlemen,

I HAVE now the honour to send you the Narrative, which I promised in my letter of the 18th October, of the transactions and events which passed during the course of the late insurrection of this province.

I had

I had begun it at the time of the date prefixed to it, but the busy scenes which followed, both while was at Chunar and after my return to Benares, hindered me from prosecuting it till a few days before the date which I have subjoined to it. I did not chuse to alter the introduction, although written at such a distance of time from that in which the body of the work was executed, and even from the existence of the events which are recorded in the latter, because I found it not easy to give it a new form, without a total omission of what had been already produced, while my mind was animated by the recent, and actual scenes on which it was engaged. To an anxious and most feeling solicitude, not more for the issue of

the

the impending conteſt, than for its conſequences on my own reputation: in the conſciouſneſs of the rectitude of my own intentions, I had allowed myſelf to uſe an appeal, the moſt ſolemn and moſt ſacred that could bind my relation to truth, or impreſs the conviction of it on the hearts of others; nor could I, conſiſtently with my own ſenſe of its obligation, withdraw it, or coldly place it after the narrative already written, and written under the check which I had impoſed upon it. I know not whether I ſhall be clearly underſtood; if I am not, yet let this endeavour to explain a ſeeming impropriety in the conſtruction of this performance be accepted for its apology.

I have

I have only to add my hope, that as I have received the moſt cordial ſupport in the paſt events from you, my reſpectable, and moſt reſpected aſſociates in the adminiſtration; and as it has been my unvaried ſtudy to prevent your ſuffering any embarraſsment from them, my conduct in them may alſo receive its firſt reward, in the teſtimomy of your approbation.

I have the honour to be, &c.

(Signed)

WARREN HASTINGS.

Benares, 31ſt Dec. 1781.

Mr. Haſtings's Narrative

OF THE LATE

TRANSACTIONS

AT

B E N A R E S.

Chunar, 1ſt of September, 1781.

IN whatever manner the ſcene may cloſe in which I am now engaged, the calamities with which it opened will not fail, in their firſt impreſſion, to influence in ſome degree the minds of all men in forming their judgment of it. In the following Narrative, if I can truſt to my own ſentiments, or if thoſe who ſhall read it will credit this declaration of them, I ſhall leſs ſtudy to efface that impreſſion than ſeek to diveſt my mind of all partial bias, and to deliver all the paſt tranſactions and occurrences with the ſtricteſt and moſt faithful regard to truth; in which if I fail, I fail unknowingly: and may the God of Truth ſo judge me, as my own conſcience ſhall condemn or acquit me of intentional deception!

The

The motives and objects of my journey were various: with these the design of my transactions at Benares had but a remote and secondary connection. I left Calcutta on the 7th of July. At Buxar, Rajah Cheit Sing paid me the customary duty of respect, by advancing to that place which lay the nearest to the boundary of his Zemidarry. He brought with him a great fleet of boats, which, as I afterwards learned, were crouded with two thousand armed and chosen men. This circumstance was noticed by many of the gentlemen who accompanied me, and was certainly a deviation from the established rules of decorum; not only such as are observed from vassals to their superiors, but even such as pass between equals. An instance of this will be remembered by many to have happened at Benares, in the year 1773, in the meeting which took place there between the late Vizier Suja ul Dowla and myself. He had left his capital with a large retinue; but hearing that I came unattended, he dismissed his followers, and met me with a state as humble as mine.

I received the Rajah with civility, and without any expression of displeasure. I left Buxar the next morning, and received a second visit from the Rajah in my boat. After a short space, he desired to speak to me in private. The particu-

lars

lars of our converſation I do not exactly remember: I can only relate the ſubſtance of it. He profeſſed much concern to hear that I was diſpleaſed with him, and contrition for having given cauſe for it, aſſuring me that his Zemidarry and all that he poſſeſſed were at my devotion: he expreſſed his fears of Ooſſaun Sing, who had been ſome days in my ſuite, and of the intrigues of his relations; and he accompanied his words by an action either ſtrongly expreſſive of the agitation of his mind, or his deſire to impreſs on mine a conviction of his ſincerity, by laying his turban on my lap. I replied, that I had not ſeen Ooſſaun Sing, nor concerned myſelf about him, nor ſhould I deſcend to be a party in his family diſagreements; that my buſineſs was with him, and with him only: that what he heard, or might have conjectured of my diſpleaſure, was true; and I entered into a full diſcuſſion of the cauſes of it; that I had been already once deceived by his oaths and proteſtations, and ſhould not ſuffer my purpoſe to be changed, or my duty to be over-ruled, by any verbal conceſſions or declarations, which were made with little coſt, and for the obſervance of which I had no pledge nor warrant to credit them. He pleaded his inability to anſwer my charges againſt him, admitted that he was in every reſpect faulty, but deſired that I would forget the paſt, and form

 my

my opinion of him on his future behaviour: I declined any further converſation on the ſubject, and he took his leave.

As the preceding converſation was accidental, and made no part of the plan which I had concerted in my own mind for my conduct with the Rajah, I kept no minutes of it, nor ſhould have thought it deſerving of a place in this narrative, but for the weight which he has ſince given to it, and that it might not be imputed to me as a deſigned ſuppreſſion, if I made no mention of it, I ſhall proceed to relate the ſubjects to which it alluded, and add the purpoſes which I had in contemplation concerning them.

On the firſt intelligence of the war with France, in July, 1778, it was reſolved in Council, that Rajah Cheit Sing ſhould be required to contribute an extraordinary ſubſidy for the expence which this new exigency had impoſed on our Government; and the ſum was limited to five Lacks of Rupees for the current year. After many excuſes, and proteſtations of inability, he at length conſented, with a very ill grace, to the payment, and with a worſe diſcharged it. The next year the ſame demand was repeated, and he attempted in like manner to elude it, affecting to borrow money in ſmall ſums, and to ſell his plate

plate and jewels to raiſe the ſum; nor was it paid at laſt till he had reduced the board to the extremity of ordering two battalions of Sepoys to the neighbourhood of Ramnagur, and quartering them upon him, with their pay charged to his account, until the whole payment was completed.

Early in the following year, about the month of May, he deputed Lalla Saddanund, who was his buxey and the confidential manager of his affairs, on a private commiſſion to me, to ſolicit my forgiveneſs for his paſt conduct, and to give me aſſurances, confirmed by oath, of his future ſubmiſſion to the orders of my government, and compliance with my advice. I accepted his excuſes, and promiſed him an oblivion of all that had paſſed exceptionable in his conduct, and my future protection and every good office in my power, ſo long as he adhered to his profeſſions: requiring only as the pledge of their ſincerity, that he would immediately notify his ready and unreſerved conſent to the demand which would be made upon him, this being the period for it, of the ſubſidy for the current year, and that he would uſe no delay in diſcharging it. I at the ſame time explained to Saddanund the nature of the demand, its conformity to the cuſtoms of all States in times of extraordinary emergency, and aſſured him that, though he muſt expect a repetition of it every year ſo long as the war laſted,

yet

yet it could not be juſtly drawn into a precedent for enacting an encreaſe on his regular and ſtipulated rent; and ſo far as it could depend upon me, I gave him the ſtrongeſt aſſurances, and I believe very ſolemn aſſeverations, that it ſhould not. Saddanund vowed the fulleſt obedience on the part of his maſter: the demand was accordingly made; and the Rajah anſwered it with a liberal and unreſerved declaration of his acquieſcence. I expected the immediate payment of the whole ſum according to his engagement, and I placed a reliance upon it ſo far as to deſtine the appropriation of it to the ſupport of the detachment, which was then acting in the Province of Malva, under the command of Lieut. Col. Camac, not apprehending any policy which could warp him from the ſtrong obligation of ſuch an engagement, and from the evident intereſt which he had in fulfilling it. I was miſtaken. The firſt payment was made in different periods in the courſe of a month, amounting to about a lack of rupees; and there, as I recollect, he ſtopped, and even deſcended to the meanneſs of writing to ſolicit the forbearance of the remainder, that it might be included in the regular payment of the enſuing year, which was then approaching. I am not poſſeſſed at this time of the materials for aſcertaining the dates of the demand, and of his letter written in acquieſcence of it, nor the dates and correſpondent ſums of the ſubſequent payments but I desire that these may be inserted by the Secretary as a note to this page of the narrative*. It is sufficient to say that the demand was made, and the whole payment consequently due, in July, that it was not until the month of October, nor until the same constraint was practised to compel his obedience as had been used in the preceding year, by an order for the advance of two battalions of Sepoys for that purpose, that the balance of the subsidy, which was two lacks and a half of rupees, was discharged. In the mean time the resident received an order from the board to remit the money, as he received it, by bills to the Pay Master of Lieut. Col. Camac's detachment; but these from the lateness of the receipts were not sent until the detachment had suffered the extremity of distress from the want of money, and very great desertions; all which calamities I charge to Rajah Cheit Sing's account, as it is certain that my reliance on his faith, and his breach of it were the principal causes that no other provision had been made for the detachment, and that it suffered such want in consequence.

It is with the greatest tenderness that I recur to the past dissentions in our Government; but I am com-

*

July — — —	100,000
August — — —	50,000
September — —	100,000
20th of October —	250,000
	500,000

compelled to it on this occasion for the elucidation of the conduct of this man, which had the appearance of being invariably guided by the reports which were made to him of the state of my influence. When he deputed his Buxey Saddanund to me in the manner I have mentioned, an apparent harmony had taken place in our Councils, with the general expectation of its being permanent. The powers of our Government whenever united, and if I may use the term, consolidated by such an event, will ever recover the respect which is due to them, especially from those who have rendered themselves obnoxious to its terrors. The subject which produced the subsequent contest between Mr. Francis and myself originated a little before the departure of Saddanund from the presidency, but was not perhaps either generally known, or known to have grown into a decided breach, till the latter end of July. A reference to the proceedings of that period will prove the grounds of this supposition. It was the prescribed duty of Cheit Sing's Vakeels to furnish him with every little anecdote which bore any relation to the state of our Government: I believe that the deliberate manner in which he made the first payment of the subsidy of that year was dictated by the doubts suggested of the firmness of my authority; and I am morally certain that his subsequent excuses and delays in the payment of the residue of the subsidy were caused by the belief that I was

no

no longer able to enforce it, and poſſibly (for ſuch was the report) that a few months would cloſe the period of my adminiſtration altogether. That I had his ſolemn promiſe in the manner which I have recited, to pay the ſubſidy, I as ſolemnly affirm; and his letter aſſenting to the payment, which is recorded in our conſultations, is a ſtrong preſumptive evidence of it; and that he evaded the performance of his promiſe, that he attempted to the utmoſt of his power to elude it altogether, is alſo proved by the record of the dates of the different payments, the minutes of the Board relating to them, and the order of the Board for the march of a detachment for the purpoſe of compelling him to perform it. That this order had a principal effect in bringing him to a compliance I believe; but I alſo attribute a ſhare of it to the approaching departure of Mr. Francis, which was publicly and generally expected.

I owe it in candour to the Gentleman, whoſe name I have reluctantly repeated in this digreſſion, to obviate any inference which might otherwiſe be unwarily drawn from it, by declaring that I mean not, by the moſt diſtant hint, to impute any of this policy to him, and in my heart do totally and deliberately acquit him of any concern in it, however, in the inſtant reſentment of diſappointment, I may have ſuffered my mind to catch ſuch a ſuſpicion, although I believe that if I have, it has been ſacredly confined to my own breaſt.

This was the firſt direct charge which I had to prefer againſt the Rajah: the ſecond was ſimilar in its quality and principle. On the ſecond of the month of November, 1780, a reſolution paſſed the Board, that a letter ſhould be written to the Nabob Vizier, adviſing him to require from the Nabob Feyz Oolla Cawn the number of troops ſtipulated by treaty, expreſſed, as they were then underſtood, to be 5000 horſe; and that the like demand ſhould be made on Rajah Cheit Sing for all the cavalry in his pay, which he could ſpare for our ſervice. At that time we ſtood in need of every aid that could be deviſed to re ell the multiplied dangers which ſurrounded us; the Rajah was ſuppoſed to maintain a very large and expenſive force; and the ſtrength of his cavalry alone was eſtimated at two thouſand. I had formerly experienced their utility in the war with the Sineaſſies, in which they were ſucceſsfully employed, and liberally rewarded. The demand was formally made, both in a letter from myſelf, and in perſon by the Reſident, Mr Fowke, in the eaſy and indefinite terms mentioned above. His anſwers were evaſive, pleading, as I recollect, for I am not in poſſeſſion of them, the ſcantineſs

of

of the eſtabliſhment, its employment in enforcing the collections, and the danger of theſe failing, if the detachments were withdrawn. At length a more peremptory order was ſent to him, and repeated by the preſent Reſident, Mr. Markham. The number required was 2000, and afterwards reduced to the demand of 1500, and laſtly to 1000; but with no more ſucceſs. He offered 250, but furniſhed none.

Theſe inſtances of contumacy and diſobedience, criminal as they were in themſelves, and aggravated by the extreme and known diſtreſſes and dangers of the ſuperior ſtate, to which he owed not only perſonal fealty, but every voluntary aid which all the reſources of his Zemidarry could contribute, appeared to me of leſs conſideration as ſuch than as they were evidences of a deliberate and ſyſtematic conduct, aiming at the total ſubverſion of the authority of the Company, and the erection of his own independency on its ruins. This had been long and generally imputed to him. It was reported that he had inherited a vaſt maſs of wealth from his father Bulwant Sing, which he had ſecured in the two ſtrong fortreſſes of Bidjeygur and Luteefpoor, and made yearly additions to it; that he kept up a large military eſtabliſhment both of cavalry, of diſciplined and irregular infantry, and of artillery; that he had the above and many other fortreſſes, of ſtrong conſtruction and in good repair, and conſtantly well ſtored and garriſoned; that his Aumils and tenants were encouraged and habituated to treat Engliſh paſſengers with inhoſpitality, and with enmity; that he maintained a correſpondence with the Marattas, and other powers who either were or might eventually become the enemies of our ſtate; and if the diſaffected Zemidars of Fyzabad and Bahar were not included in the report, which I do not recollect, we have had woeful proof that there was equal room to have ſuſpected the like intercourſe between them; and laſtly, that he was collecting, or had prepared, every proviſion for open revolt, waiting only for a proper ſeaſon to declare it, which was ſuppoſed to depend either on the arrival of a French armament, or on a Maratta invaſion.

This deſign had been greatly favoured by the unhappy diviſions of our government, in which he preſumed to take an open part. It is a fact, that when theſe had proceeded to an extremity bordering on civil violence, by the attempt to wreſt from me my authority in the month of June, 1777, he had deputed a man, named Sumboonaut, with an expreſs commiſſion to my opponent; and the man had proceeded as far as Moorſhedabad, when hearing of the change of

affairs

affairs which had taken place at the Prefidency, he ftopped, and the Rajah recalled him.

It may, perhaps, be urged in favour of Rajah Cheit Sing, that he was juftifiable by the principle of good policy in feeking a ftate of independency; that we had no natural right to his vaffalage, having acquired it, with all our other rights of dominion, by no other charter than the fuccefsful fpirit of enterprize. Were this truly the cafe, it would reduce the relation between us to the primitive law of nature; and it would be equally incumbent on us on that ground alone to ufe every means to confirm and perpetuate his fubjection, as it would be allowable in him to emancipate himfelf from it. But fomething more, I apprehend, was due, both as a political and even moral obligation from him. His father, Bulwant Sing, derived the degree of independency which he poffeffed during the latter period of his life, from the protection and intervention of our government. His fon, Cheit Sing, obtained from our influence, exerted by myfelf, the firft legal title that his family ever poffeffed of property in the land, of which he, till then, was only the Aumil, and of which he became the acknowledged Zemidar, by a Sunnud granted to him by the Nabob Suja ul Dowla, at my inftance, in the month of September, 1773. On the fucceffion ſion of the Nabob Aſſof ul Dowla, the rights of ſovereignty, which were held by him over the Zemidarry, were transferred by treaty to the Company. Thoſe rights were indiſputably his, and became, by his alienation of them, as indiſputably the Company's; and every obligation of fidelity and obedience, which is due from a Zemidar to the ſuperior magiſtrates by the conſtitution of Hindoſtan, became as much the right of the Company from Cheit Sing, as they had been due to his former ſovereign, with the additional ties of gratitude for the ſuperior advantages which he was allowed to poſſeſs with his new relation. The unexampled lenity of our government, in relinquiſhing to him the free and uncontrouled rule of his Zemidarry, ſubject to a limited annual fine, and the royalties of the mint, adminiſtration of juſtice and police, ought to have operated as an additional claim on his fidelity; but evidently ſerved but to ſtimulate his ambition, and perhaps to excite in his mind an opinion that he poſſeſſed an inherent right of ſelf-dependency.

I conſidered Cheit Sing as culpable, in a very high degree, towards our ſtate, and his puniſhment, of which I had given him frequent warnings if he did not amend his conduct, as an example which juſtice and policy required, equally for the reparation of the wrongs which its dignity

had

had sustained, and for the future preservation of its authority. I was resolved to draw from his guilt the means of relief to the Company's distresses, and to exact a penalty, which I was convinced he was very able to bear, from a fund which I was also convinced he had destined for purposes of the most dangerous tendency to the Company's dominion. In a word, I had determined to make him pay largely for his pardon, or to exact a severe vengeance for his past delinquency.

Those who have been accustomed to regard Cheit Sing as a vassal, or tributary prince, may revolt at the idea of treating him with such indignity, and call it an oppression. They will suppose nothing due from him to the Company but the payment of his stipulated tribute, and *that* the pledge of his exemption from every other claim. I suspect too that the deeds, which passed between him and the Board on the transfer of his Zemidarry to the Company in 1775, are by many understood to bear the quality and force of a treaty of optional conditions between equal states.—To such I reply, that such an opinion is itself criminal to the state of which he was a subject, and that he was himself amenable to its justice if he gave countenance to the belief. He paid no tribute to the Company, but a fixed annual rent.

The

The deeds by which he held his Zemidarry, and the Company their claim to their portion of its revenue, were a Sunnud, or grant, and a Potta, or leafe, executed on the part of the Company; and a Cabuleeat, or agreement, and Kiftbundee, or account of payments to be made by inftallments, on his part. Thefe, excepting the fpecial privileges allowed to the Rajah of the Mint, the Cutwallees of Benares and Jowanpoor, the Foojdarree and Aumeeny; that is, fo far as they relate to the Zemidarry alone, are drawn precifely in the fame forms as inftruments of the fame denominations interchanged with the Zemidars of Bengal. I refer to the inftruments themfelves, which will make a number in the Appendix to this Narrative, in which it will be feen on how different a tenure, and how infinitely below independency, he really held his Zemidarry. The Sunnud and Cabuleeat are exact counterparts of each other. The former prefcribes the revenue which was to be paid, and the duties which were to be performed, as the conditions on which the Rajah was confirmed in the poffeffion of his Zemidarry; and of thefe conditions the Cabuleeat is a pledge or engagement for the performance. In the firft, the "government and fovereignty" of the Zemidarry, transferred by the Nabob Affof ul Dowla to the Company, are ftated as the bafis of is The Zemidarry is confirmed to him: A

ftrict

ſtrict "obſervation and execution of the duties in-"cumbent on him;"—"to behave with modera-"tion and kindneſs to the Reyots and people; to "promote the cultivation and increaſe of the in-"habitants and produce of the lands;" to preſerve the peace, and "puniſh the diſturbers of "it;" and to pay a yearly rent of 2,340,249 Mahidar rupees, in monthly payments, agreeable to the Kiſtbundy; are moſt ſtrictly and poſitively commanded and enjoined:——And the officers of the Zemidarry are commanded to regard him as the Zemidar, "and to acknowledge his autho-"rity in the ſeveral acts appertaining thereunto." ——I muſt obſerve that, in the tranſlation of the Sunnud, the yearly revenue is in one place, through the negligence of the tranſlator, expreſſed by the word tribute: but it is not on the tranſlation, nor on the will of the tranſlator, that the rights of the Company depend. I affirm the word to be falſe, as it is inconſiſtent with the proper term "revenue," immediately following in the ſame tranſlation. and with the ſame term "revenue," occurring in the tranſlation of the Cabuleeat or agreement.

The Cabuleeat alſo ſets off with ſtating the Company's ſovereignty as the baſis of the agreement; and acknowledges the grant made by the Company to Rajah Cheit Sing, of the Zemidarry and other privileges recited in the Sunnud. And it proceeds to expreſs, that " it ſhall be his duty " to do every thing that may be needful and uſual " for the intereſt and ſecurity of the country; to " provide for the welfare of the inhabitants; to " be attentive to the encreaſe of cultivation and " improvement of the revenue; to uſe his en- " deavours " to expel robbers," &c. and to pay the " annual revenue of government, in the manner " preſcribed by the Sunnud."

To obviate miſapprehenſions I think it proper to remark, that in the above recital I have abridged the text where it was too prolix and involved for literal quotation, and given the ſubſtance in the cloſeſt ſenſe of it; but where I have uſed the original words of the tranſlations, I have marked them with inverted commas as ſuch. The copies in the Appendix will ſhew with what fidelity I have conformed to the text in both inſtances.

I have dwelt with a greater ſtreſs, and with a more minute exactneſs on the foregoing ſubject, becauſe it is on this point that the juſtice and propriety of my conduct muſt wholly turn. If Rajah Cheit Sing poſſeſſed the Zemidarry of Benares in his own right, and with an inherent and excluſive authority; if he owed no allegiance to the Company, nor obedience beyond the payments of a

ſtipulated

ſtipulated tribute, I am liable to condemnation for exacting other duties from him, and for all the conſequences of that exaction, and he is guiltleſs. But if the Company, poſſeſſing the acknowledged right of his former Sovereign, held an abſolute authority over him; if in the known relation of Zemidar to the ſovereign authority, or the power delegated by it, he owed a perſonal allegiance and an implicit and unreſerved obedience to that authority; at the forfeiture of his Zemidarry, and even of his life and property, at the diſcretion of thoſe who held or fully repreſented the ſovereign authority; if, in corroboration of the general and implied obligation, he was bound to it by written engagements and ſpecific conditions, I am warranted in my aſſertion of the rights of government, which were fully and wholly delegated to me; and he alone is reſponſible for his oppoſition to them, and for all the conſequences which have attended that oppoſition.

Whether I have exerciſed the power veſted in me with juſtice, and with moderation, will appear from the preceding relation, and the following parts of this narrative.

Before I quit this digreſſion, I muſt further treſpaſs on the patience of the Board, and of thoſe for whoſe judgment it is ultimately written, by a more pointed application of the above to my own perſonal conduct and character.

I will ſuppoſe for a moment that I have erred, that I have acted with an unwarranted rigour towards Cheit Sing, and even with injuſtice. Let my motive be conſulted: I left Calcutta impreſſed with the belief that extraordinary means were neceſſary, and thoſe exerted with a ſtrong hand, to preſerve the Company's intereſts from ſinking under the accumulated weight which oppreſſed them: I ſaw a political neceſſity for curbing the overgrown power of a great member of their dominion, and for making it contribute to the relief of their preſſing exigencies.

If I erred, my error was prompted by an exceſs of zeal for their intereſts operating with too ſtrong a bias upon my judgment. But rare are the inſtances in which the judgment ſuffers the bias of ſuch an operation; and much ſtronger is the preſumption, that acts prompted by an unmixed attention to the public intereſts are founded on juſt principles, than that they are the reſult of a miſguided judgment.

Poſſibly it may be ſuſpected, and may God forgive thoſe who know me, and countenance the ſuſpicion, I have no title to an exemption from it

with

with others, that I was influenced by a ſecret and mercenary intereſt. I have heard of the practice of holding out the terrors of authority, and the denunciations of diſgrace, diſmiſſion, and war, as the inſtruments of private rapacity. Though the charge, if true, is capable of poſitive conviction, yet I know of no direct evidence which could refute it where it were falſe ; for no man can be conſcious of the receſſes of another's mind. I can therefore only offer ſuch preſumptive proofs of my intention as the nature of it will admit, and accident has provided. Theſe are my own early and confidential declarations, and the atteſtations of thoſe to whom they were made. In a point of ſuch public moment, independently of the near intereſt which I have in eſtabliſhing the truth of it, Mr. Wheler will pardon my appeal to him, although in one light it may tend to involve him in a participation of the reproach of thoſe who may regard every ſeverity ſhewn to Cheit Sing as criminal, however founded. He will doubtleſs recollect the converſation which I had with him on the ſubject, on the eve of my departure from Calcutta ; our mutual opinion of Cheit Sing's paſt conduct ; mine of the juſtice and policy of exacting an exemplary puniſhment for it by a large pecuniary mulct ; the ſum to which I then declared my reſolution to extend it ; my conviction of his ability to pay it ; and the two alternatives on which

I had

I had resolved, if he refused to submit to it. He will also remember that I bespoke his confidence in the means which I should use for this end, and his support in the issue of them. I entreat him to give me his formal and circumstantial attestation of these facts, and that he will permit it to be inserted in this part of my narrative.

" I have the pleasure to comply with the Go-
" vernor-General's request, and will chearfully
" record in this place what I at present recollect to
" have passed between us at the time, and on the
" circumstances which he mentions. I well re-
" member, that on the eve of the Governor-Gene-
" ral's departure from Calcutta, the conduct of
" Cheit Sing, late Rajah of Benares, was a principal
" subject of a confidential discourse between us,
" and that he bespoke my support of the measures
" which he intended to pursue towards him.

" The Rajah's offences were declared to require
" early punishment, and as his wealth was great,
" and the company's exigencies pressing, it was
" thought a measure of policy and justice, to exact
" from him a large pecuniary mulct for their re-
" lief. The sum to which the Governor declared
" his resolution to extend this fine, was forty or
" fifty lacks. His ability to pay it was stated as a
" fact that could not admit of doubt, and the two

alternatives

" alternatives on which the Governor declared
" himſelf to have reſolved, if Cheit Sing refuſed to
" comply with the requiſition, were, to the beſt of
" my remembrance, either a removal from his
" Zemidary entirely, or by taking poſſeſſion of
" his forts, to obtain out of the treaſure depoſited
" in it the above ſum for the Company.

EDWARD WHELER."

After ſuch an appeal it would be as ſuperfluous as indelicate to call on the aid of other teſtimonies, if all that were required were no more than to aſcertain that I did hold ſuch a converſation as that which I allude to with him. The concluſion will be much ſtrengthened by its agreement with declarations made by me on the ſame ſubject, and nearly at the ſame point of time, to others. I ſhall therefore require ſimilar atteſtations from Major Palmer, my military Secretary, and from Mr. Anderſon, my appointed aſſiſtant on this deputation. With theſe references, and their reſult, I ſhall make my laſt and ſolemn appeal to the breaſt of every man who ſhall read this; whether it is likely, or morally poſſible, that I ſhould have tied down my own future conduct to ſo decided a proceſs and ſeries of acts, if I had ſecretly intended to threaten, or to uſe a degree of violence, for no other purpoſe than to draw from the object of it a mercenary atonement for my own private emolument, and ſuffer

all

all this tumult to terminate in an oſtenſible and unſubſtantial ſubmiſſion to the authority which I repreſented? Whether it is likely, or morally poſſible, that I ſhould have choſen to irritate the feelings of my colleague in office, and expoſe myſelf to all the effects of his indignation, by ſo wanton and unneceſſary a deception; or lower my own dignity and character, and afford ſo baſe an example to my inferiors, by pretending to make them privy to acts which I never meant to perform, and from which I could not depart with any poſſible ſhew of reaſon, but the manifeſt ſacrifice of my integrity? A man actuated by ſuch a motive, and poſſeſſing the truſt which I held, would have uſed a cover to his venality: he would not have compromiſed himſelf by poſitive declarations of what he would do, much leſs by detailing his intentions in a ſeries of trials as they might ſucceſſively fail; but would have been content with diſtant and indefinite intimations and ſuggeſtions, which obviouſly left his actions open to enquiry and variation; which could not ſubject him to the imputation of inconſiſtency, if they were productive of no effect; and which he might uſe as juſtifications, if his artifices ſhould chance to operate with the effect oſtenſibly portended by them.

I now return to my narrative.

I arrived at Benares on the morning of the 14th of Auguſt; the Rajah ſome hours later. I forbad his

his coming that evening to my quarters as he had intended, and required him to defer his future visits until he should receive my permission, as I had some previous matters to settle with him, of which he would be informed by the Resident, whom I should depute to him the next morning for that purpose.

My narrative will be best continued, nor will the thread of it be broken, by the following copy of my report of my proceedings, and the consequences which attended them to Mr. Wheler, then the only effective member of the Board.

To EDWARD WHELER, Esq.

" SIR,

" I arrived at Benares on the 14th instant.
" My transactions with the Rajah being of a most
" important nature to the present and future inte-
" rests of the Company, I have determined to
" inform you of them without delay, in the order
" in which they have occurred.

" The first step which I judged it necessary to
" take, as the ground on which my future pro-
" ceedings with the Rajah were to be conducted,

" was to recapitulate in writing the ſeveral in-
" ſtances of his conduct which for ſome time paſt
" have repeatedly drawn upon him the ſevere re-
" prehenſions of the Board, and to demand a clear
" and ſatisfactory explanation.

" This paper I ſent to the Rajah by the hands
" of Mr. Markham, who was directed to require
" an immediate anſwer. Late in the evening his
" anſwer arrived. The following are copies of
" both:

" To Rajah CHEIT SING.

" It is about ſixteen months ſince Lalla Sadda-
" nund, your Buxey and confidential ſervant,
" came to Calcutta, charged with an expreſs com-
" miſſion and authority to make excuſes for your
" paſt conduct, and to give me aſſurances, con-
" firmed by oath, of your future ſubmiſſion to
" my advice and the orders of my government.
" As a teſt of your ſincerity, I required an imme-
" diate and unreſerved acquieſcence in the demand,
" which at the ſame time was made to you in the
" the name of the Governer General and Council,
" of a ſubſidy of five lacks of rupees for the ex-
" pences of the war. With this demand you
" oſtenſibly complied, in your anſwer to my
" letter;

" letter; and the Buxey promised me verbally in " your name, and in terms so strong as amounted " to the fullest assurance, that there should be no " delay in the payment. Relying on this agree- " ment and promise, I gave orders to Mr. Fowke, " who was then Resident at this place, to re- " ceive the money, and remit it to Colonel Camac, " for the pay of the army which had been " ordered to march towards the Province of " Malva, and I made no other provision for it. " Such was my confidence in your faith, but you " deceived me; and after having made the first " payment of a few rupees, either consulting " the temper of the times, or conforming to a " premeditated design, you by shifts and pretexts " with-held the remainder until the army, for " whose use it was intended, was reduced to the " last state of distress: many hundreds deserted, " and had an enemy at that time appeared against " them, their total destruction had been inevitable. " In all this time daily application was made to " you by the Resident, and I wrote repeated let- " ters to you, but you paid no regard to either. " Besides this, I required in the name of the Go- " vernor General and Council by letter, and " ordered Mr Fowke to repeat the requisition in " person, that you should furnish a body of horse " to assist and act with the armies of the Company; " and, when Mr. Markham succeeded Mr. Fowke,

 " I gave

"I gave him an order to repeat the demand, "which he did accordingly with frequent and "almoſt daily importunity, limiting the num- "ber to 1500, and afterwards to 1000. To this "demand you returned evaſive anſwers, nor to "this hour have you contributed a ſingle horſe- "man.

"I paſs over other inſtances of your conduct, "in which, through the means of your ſecret "agents, you have endeavoured to excite diſorders "in the government on which you depend; and "your neglect of the duty which you owe to it, "and to the ſubjects of this Zemidarry, by ſuffer- "ing the daily perpetration of robberies and mur- "ders, even in the ſtreets of the city of Benares "itſelf, to the great and public ſcandal of the "Engliſh name, and in violation of one of the "conditions on which you received the confirma- "tion of this Zemidarry. But as the two fore- "going inſtances amount to a direct charge of "diſaffection and infidelity to the government on "which you depend, and happened at a time in "which it was your duty more eſpecially to have "exerted yourſelf in the ſupport of its intereſts, "I have therefore judged it proper to ſtate them "to you thus fully in writing, and to require "your anſwer to them; and this I expect imme- "diately."

From

From Rajah CHEIT SING to the Honourable the GOVERNOR GENERAL.

" I received your letter delivered to me by Mr.
" Markham, and I have underftood every parti-
" cular of its contents. Sir, after the arrival of
" Shaick Ally Nucky, I obferved all the orders
" which you fent me, and I received the letter
" which the deceafed Shaick brought me, inform-
" ing me that every fufpicion was now completely
" removed from your mind, and that I muft confi-
" der you as formerly attentive to me : but I have
" not experienced from you the fame generofities
" as formerly. I fent you repeatedly letters re-
" prefenting to your confideration my unhappy
" circumftances, but you never honoured me with
" any reply. For this reafon I fent my Buxey Sad-
" danund to your prefence, enjoining him to re-
" prefent to you the firmnefs of my obedience and
" attachment, to lay before you the particulars of
" my fituation, and to learn the difpofition of your
" mind towards me. He arrived accordingly in
" your prefence, and reprefented every thing in
" a proper manner. I have never deviated in
" the fmalleft degree from thefe profeffions ; and
" the benefits and civilities with which you have
" honoured me have given me the greateft fatis-
" faction, and I have confidered you as the fource
" from which I derived the fulfillment of all my
" wifhes

" wishes and desires. It is my firm hope that I " may be always favoured with your directions. " In this manner I complied with the utmost readiness with the order you sent me for the payment of five lacks of rupees on account of the " expences of the war. I sent first one lack of " rupees, with an answer to your letter; afterwards " having paid to Mr. Fowke the sum of one lack " and 70,000 rupees, I sent a letter requesting a " further allowance of time to enable me to make " some preparations. To this I received no " reply; it being no time for delay. Notwithstanding this, I was not a moment inattentive " to this concern, and as soon as my Buxey arrived, I paid immediately the remaining part of " the sum. The remitting of this to the army " did not depend on me: if any delay happened " on this head, I could not help it. If besides the " payment of the money, the remittance of it " also to the army had rested with me, a delay " of this kind should not have happened. I have " inclosed in this letter a paper specifying the particular sums which have been advanced, with " their dates.

" With respect to the horse, you desired me in " your letter to inform you what number I could " afford to station with you, and I sent you a particular account of all that were in my service,

" amounting

" amounting to 1200 horſe, of which ſeveral were " ſtationed at diſtant places; but I received no " anſwer to this. Mr. Markham delivered me an " order to prepare 1000 horſe. In compliance " with your wiſhes I collected 500 horſe, and as " a ſubſtitute for the remainder, 500 burkundoſſes, " of which I ſent you information, and I told Mr. " Markham they were ready to go to whatever " place they ſhould be ſent. No anſwer, however, " came from you on this head, and I remained " aſtoniſhed at the cauſe of it. Repeatedly I " aſked Mr. Markham about an anſwer to my let- " ter about the horſe, but he told me he did not " know the reaſons of no anſwer having been ſent. " I remained aſtoniſhed. With reſpect to the " ſepoys, I received firſt an order to ſtation two " of my companies, which I did: I was then de- " ſired to give a Tunkaw for the payment of the " ſepoys, and likewiſe to pay the Captain, which " has been done every month.

" Excepting Abdullah Beg and his attendants, " none of my people, either dependants or ſervants, " or others in any ſhape connected with me, have " ever gone to Calcutta: my enemies, with a view " to my ruin, have made falſe repreſentations to " you. Now that happily for me you have yourſelf " arrived at this place, you will be able to aſcertain " all the circumſtances relative to the horſe, to

" my

"my people going to Calcutta, and the dates of "the receipts of the particular ſums above-men- "tioned. You will know whether I have amuſed "you with a falſe repreſentation, or made a juſt "report to you. I have given my Aumils moſt "particular injunctions, and have taken a penalty "bond from them, that they ſhall keep no thieves "in their diſtrict. What power have they to act "otherwiſe? But if ever a murder or robbery is "committed in the country, I have been careful "to impale or otherwiſe puniſh the culprit. If a "perſon having committed a delinquency ſhould "eſcape to ſome other place, ſo as to elude all dif- "covery, in that caſe I am helpleſs; but to the "utmoſt of my power I endeavour to fulfil your "orders. I have never ſwerved in the ſmalleſt "degree from my duty to you. It remains with "you to decide on all theſe matters. I am in "every caſe your ſlave; what is juſt I have re- "preſented to you: may your proſpeirty increaſe."

"Account of five lacks of rupees advanced for the expences of the war.

1ſt	Shaabaun	100,000
29th	Ramzan	170,000
7th	Showull	130,000
18th	Showull	100,000
		500,000

"This

" This anſwer you will perceive to be not " only unſatisfactory in ſubſtance, but offenſive " in ſtile, and leſs a vindication of himſelf than a " recrimination on me. It expreſſes no concern " for the cauſes of complaint contained in my " letter, or deſire to atone for them, nor the " ſmalleſt intention to purſue a different line of " conduct. An anſwer couched nearly in terms " of defiance to requiſitions of ſo ſerious a nature, " I could not but conſider as a ſtrong indication " of that ſpirit of independency which the Rajah " has for ſome years paſt aſſumed, and of which " indeed I had early obſerved other manifeſt " ſymptoms, both before and from the inſtant " of my arrival.

" Under theſe alarming appearances of the " Rajah's conduct and diſpoſition, I conceived " myſelf indiſpenſibly obliged to form ſome im-" mediate and deciſive plan for obviating their " conſequences, and for the preſervation of the " Company's rights and intereſts in this Zemi-" darry. To have left him in the full exerciſe of " powers which he had notoriouſly abuſed, and " which it was to be apprehended he would " employ to the moſt dangerous purpoſes, was to-" tally inconſiſtent with the maxims of juſtice and " prudence. To diveſt him entirely of the Ze-" midarry, though juſtifiable on the grounds ſtated

" above, would have been attended with an
" appearance of severity, and might have fur-
" nished ground for constructions unfavourable
" to the credit of our government, and to my
" own reputation, from the natural influence
" which every act of rigour exercised on the per-
" sons of men who stand in elevated stations,
" is apt to impress on the minds of those who
" are too remote from the scene of action to
" judge, by any evidence but of the direct facts
" themselves, of their motives or propriety.

" Thus circumstanced, and attentive to these
" opposite considerations, I laid down the follow-
" ing plan for my future proceedings :

" I first directed the Resident to repair to the
" *Rajah*, who resided at his house, situated on
" this side of the river, at the distance of about
" two miles, and gave him the following in-
" structions :

" Mr. WILLIAM MARKHAM,
" Resident at *Benares*.

" SIR,

" It is my order that you proceed early to-mor-
" row morning to the house of Rajah Cheit Sing,
" with your usual guard, and put him in arrest.
" You

" You will require his immediate submission, informing him that you act under orders given you by me; and in case of his refusal, you will wait the arrival of two companies of sepoys belonging to Major Popham's detachment, who are directed to follow and assist you in the execution of this service. Having secured the Rajah, you will keep him in your custody until further orders. I am, &c.

" *Benares, 15th of August, 1781,*
" *ten at night.*"

" On the next morning Mr. Markham went according to his foregoing instructions, and was followed by two companies of grenadier sepoys belonging to Major Popham's detachment. The Rajah quietly submitted to the arrest, and Mr. Markham returned to me with the following letter from the Rajah, leaving him under the charge of Lieutenants Stalker, Scott, and Simes. For the particulars which passed at this interview, I refer you to the following report, which Mr. Markham delivered to me on his return.

" No. IV. Letter from Rajah CHEIT SING.

" At this time Mr. William Markham being come to me, has informed me that your Highness's orders are that I shonld remain under a

 " guard.

" guard. My Protector, I before represented to
" you, on board your pinnace, that I was the
" servant of the Honourable Company, and was
" ready from my heart and soul. Whatever
" may be your pleasure, do it with your own
" hands. I am your slave. What occasion can
" there be for a guard?

" No. V. Report of Mr. MARKHAM.

" To the Honourable WARREN HASTINGS, Esq.
" Governor-general, &c. &c.

" Honourable Sir,

" I this morning, in obedience to your orders
" of last night, proceeded with a few of my Or-
" derlies, accompanied by Lieutenant Stalker, to
" Shewallah Gaut, the present residence of Rajah
" Cheit Sing, and acquainted him it was your
" pleasure he should consider himself in arrest,
" that he should order his people to behave in a
" quiet, orderly manner, for that any attempt
" to rescue him would be attended with his own
" destruction. The Rajah submitted quietly to
" the arrest, and assured me that whatever were
" your orders, he was ready implicitly to obey.
" He hoped that you would allow him a sub-
" sistence; but as for his Zemidarry, his forts,
" and his treasure, he was ready to lay them at

" your

" your feet, and his life, if required. He ex-
" preſſed himſelf much hurt at the ignominy
" which he affirmed muſt be the conſequence of
" his confinement, and entreated me to return to
" you with the foregoing ſubmiſſion, hoping that
" you would make allowances for his youth and
" inexperience, and, in conſideration of his father's
" name, releaſe him from his confinement as ſoon
" as he ſhould prove the ſincerity of his offers,
" and himſelf deſerving of your compaſſion and
" forgiveneſs.

" Nearly a quarter of an hour after this con-
" verſation, Lieut. Scott arrived with the two
" grenadier companies of Major Popham's de-
" tachment, to whoſe and Lieutenant Stalker's
" care I left the Rajah, having given them the
" following inſtructions; that they ſhould diſarm
" every ſervant of the Rajah's, that they ſhould
" allow him any ſuch eight or ten Kiſtmutgars for
" the attendance of his perſon as he ſhould ap-
" prove of; that theſe men ſhould be ſhewn to the
" ſepoys, leſt any deceit ſhould be practiſed; but
" that they might indulge him in any requeſt con-
" ſiſtent with the ſecurity of his perſon.

" I am now returned to acquaint you with
" my proceedings, and to receive any further
" inſtructions

" instructions which you may think necessary.

" I have the honour to be,
" Honourable Sir,
" Your most obedient humble servant,
" (Signed) WILLIAM MARKHAM.

" *Benares, 16th of August*, 1781.

" As the Rajah, in the above letter, had desired " that Mr. Markham might be sent back to him, " I was preparing instructions for that purpose, " when I received another letter from the Rajah, " of which the following is a translation:

" No. VI. Letter from the Rajah.

" I am the servant of the Sirkar, and am ready " from my heart and soul in the performance of " your orders. My honour was bestowed on me " by your Highness. It depends on you alone " to take away or not to take away the country " out of my hands. In case my honour is not " left me, how shall I be equal to the business of " the Sirkar? Whoever with his hands in a supplicating posture is ready with his life and property, what necessity can there be for him to be " dealt with in this way?—

" From

" From the apparent despondency in which " these letters were written, I thought it necessary " to give the Rajah some encouragement, and " accordingly wrote him the following answer:

" No. VII. Letter from the Governor-general.

" I have received your two Arzees from the " hands of Mr. Markham, and understand their " contents. That gentleman will wait on you " in the afternoon, and explain particulars. Let " your mind be at rest, and do not conceive any " terror or apprehension.

" To this I received the following reply:

" No. VIII. Letter from the Rajah.

" Your gracious letter has been received, and " has made me acquainted with your commands. " Your order that in the afternoon Mr. William " Markham will come to me, that I must not " suffer any apprehension to disturb me, but " remain at ease in my mind. My Protector, " wherever you spread your shadow over my " head, I am entirely free from concern and " apprehension; and whatever you who are my " master shall as such determine, will be right.

" At

"At this time I had prepared Mr. Markham's
" second instructions; but before he could set out
" with them, intelligence came that large bodies
" of armed men had crossed the river from Ram-
" nagur, and had proceeded to the Rajah's house.
" What follows is a scene of such horror, that it
" is with the greatest reluctance I submit to the
" painful duty of relating it. The guard placed
" over the Rajah consisted of two companies of
" grenadier sepoys, as above mentioned, from
" Major Popham's detachment, commanded by
" the officers already named, who were stationed
" in an enclosed square, which surrounded the
" apartment where the Rajah was. The Resident's
" guard had returned with him. It now appeared
" that these troops had taken no ammunition with
" them. Major Popham sent another company
" of sepoys under an officer, with ammunition to
" reinforce and support the first party. When
" the latter arrived at the Rajah's house, they found
" it surrounded, and all the avenues blockaded,
" by a multitude of armed men, who opposed their
" passage. The minds of this tumultuous assembly
" becoming soon inflamed, some of them began to
" fire upon the sepoys within the square, and im-
" mediately, as if this had been the concerted sig-
" nal, made an instantaneous and fierce attack on
" the sepoys, who, wanting their accustomed
" means of defence, were capable of making but
" a feeble

" a feeble resistance, and fell an easy sacrifice to " the superior number of their assailants, who cut " almost every man of this unfortunate party to " pieces. The officers, it is supposed, were the " first victims to their fury, but not until they " had, by astonishing efforts of bravery, and undis- " mayed amidst the imminent dangers which sur- " rounded them, involved a much superior num- " ber of their enemies in their fate. In this gene- " ral report of them all accounts concur, though " varying in circumstances. I yield to my own " feelings in bestowing this just but unavailing " tribute to these unhappy gentlemen.

" In the midst of this confusion the Rajah " found means to escape through a wicket which " opened to the river; and the banks being ex- " ceedingly steep in that place, he let himself down " by turbans tied together, into a boat which was " waiting for him, and conveyed him to the op- " posite shore. Those who had effected his " escape, followed him across the river in the " same tumultuous manner in which they had " assembled, leaving the party of our sepoys which " had last arrived in possession of the house. On " the first intelligence of this commotion, I had " directed Major Popham to repair immediately " to his camp, which was about two miles from " the Resident's, and at the same distance from

 " the

" the Rajah's houſe, and to march inſtantly with the
" remainder of his detachment to the ſupport of
" the party.

" This order was executed with all poſſible ex-
" pedition; but Major Popham arrived too late,
" and had the mortification to be a ſpectator of
" the effects of a maſſacre which he could neither
" prevent nor revenge. He returned to me im-
" mediately, and made the following report:

" No. IX. Major Popham's Report.

" Conſequent to an order for the detachment
" under my command to proceed to the ſupport
" of the grenadier companies under the order of
" Lieut. Stalker, I carried it with as much expe-
" dition as poſſible to Cheit Sing's palace, which
" I found to be entirely evacuated by the Rajah's
" people, who were already landed on the oppo-
" ſite ſide of the river.

" Of the two companies commanded by Lieut.
" Stalker, very few remained alive, and the ma-
" jority of thoſe appeared to be ſeverely wounded.
" The bodies of Lieuts. Stalker, Scott, and Simes,
" were lying within a ſmall diſtance of each other,
" ſhockingly mangled, and without any ſigns of
" life.

" It

" It may be neceſſary to obſerve, that Lieut. " Birrell was diſpatched with one company of " ſepoys upon the firſt rumor of the Rajah's " coercive intentions; but the fate of the com- " panies which preceded him was decided prior " to his being able to enter the palace. There " were however ſome of the Rajah's people, whom " he effectually cleared it of. In his attack he " met with ſome loſs. My utmoſt endeavours " have hitherto proved inſufficient to procure an " exact detail of the killed and wounded in this " unfortunate tranſaction. I thought it neceſſary " to leave a company with a ſubaltern in the " palace."

(Signed)

WILLIAM POPHAM, Major."

" *Benares, 16th of Auguſt,* 1781."

" I cannot learn with certainty what is be- " come of the Rajah, but the prevailing report is " that he fled from Ramnagur, his uſual reſidence " on the other ſide of the river, in the middle of " the night, and proceeded with his *Zenâna* and " effects to Lutteefgur, a ſtrong fort of his, ſituate " about 10 miles from Chunar. He was ac- " companied by Sujan Sing, his brother, and " Mannyar Sing, a relation, and ſon by adoption " of Rajah Bulwant Sing. He has alſo had the

" precaution to take with him Ranny Golab-
" koower, the widow of Rajah Bulwant Sing his
" father; her ſon in law, Dwegbijey Sing; and
" his two ſons, her grandſons. In them he
" poſſeſſes every member of his family who can
" have any plea to diſpute with him the right of
" inheritance from his father Rajah Bulwant
" Sing, if that were ever a queſtion, his right to
" the Zemidarry being derived excluſively from
" Sunnuds which his father never poſſeſſed, but
" which were firſt granted to Cheit Sing by the
" late Vizier Suja ul Dowla through the influence
" of our Government in 1773, and ſince repeated
" by ſimilar grants from our Government, when
" the ſovereignty was ceded to the Company by
" the preſent Nabob Aſſof ul Dowla.

" I have made choice of Bauboo Ooſſaun
" Sing, who held the office of Dewan during ſe-
" veral years of the life of Rajah Bulwant Sing,
" and for a conſiderable period ſince the acceſſion
" of the preſent Rajah, to adminiſter the revenues
" and Government of this country in the quality
" of Naib, until it can be determined to whom
" the Zemidarry may legally belong, and who
" may be in a capacity to receive it.

" To this effect I have cauſed a proclamation
" to be made through the city of Benares, and

" have

" have notified it by circular perwannahs to all " the zemindars and aumils of the Zemidarry.

" To enforce the execution of theſe acts, to " maintain tranquility and order in the country; " and protect the inhabitants, I have ordered one " battalion of ſepoys from Chunargur, the re- " mainder of Major Popham's detachment from " Mirzapore, and one regiment of ſepoys from " Dinapore to march immediately to Benares,

" The detail of theſe proceedings ſhall be " tranſmitted to you in a ſubſequent letter. I do " not expect they will detain me here much be- " yond the time I had preſcribed to myſelf, which " was about 7 or 8 days.

" I have the honor to be, with the greateſt " eſteem,

" SIR,

" Your moſt obedient

" Humble Servant,

(Signed) WARREN HASTINGS."

" P.S. The delay occaſioned in copying this " letter from its great length has afforded me an " opportunity of contradicting the latter part of " it; and I have now the ſatisfaction to add, that

" Ranny

" Ranny Golabkoower, together with her ſon in
" law Durgbijey Sing, and his two ſons, are ſafe
" at Benares. I have this morning received a
" viſit from Durgbijey Sing, and his eldeſt ſon
" Mehipnarain."

I have read over the preceding letter with great attention, but can find nothing in it, with the advantage of recent and better means of information, to correct; nor do I know that it requires a comment. That which I am now about to make may appear trivial; but I make it as it impels me by its preſent impreſſion. The Rajah, in his reply to the charges which I had preferred againſt him, inſiſts much on the many letters which he wrote to me, praying to be diſpenſed from his obedience to the orders of Government, and my neglect to anſwer them: and this charge againſt me he repeats in a manner not the moſt reſpectful. I do not know but it may be true. He had received poſitive orders, and thoſe had been repeated. It was his duty to obey them, not to waſte my time with letters of excuſe, to cavil with my anſwers for evaſions, or with my ſilence for delays. His Vakeel was in daily attendance on me, and knew my mind ſufficiently upon theſe ſubjects; and what he knew I am ſure he wrote to his maſter. As to his plea of inability to pay the reſidue of the ſubſidy " without pre-

" paration;"

paration," that is, without contriving the means to raiſe the money, after having ſacredly promiſed the full and inſtant diſcharge of it, it was as inſolent, as we now know too ſurely, that it was moſt egregiouſly falſe.

It was truly reported that Cheit Sing, after his eſcape from Shewallah Gaut, immediately fled to Lutteefpoor, taking his family, and his whole force with him, except the ordinary guard which had been early appropriated in the time of his father, Bulwant Sing, under the command of Gudgerauge Sing, who had the title of Kellidar, to the charge of Ramnagur. This was a vaſt pile of irregular but maſſy buildings conſtructed of ſtone, on the river ſide, and within the bed of the river. To its original ſtrength Cheit Sing had added ſome ſmall baſtions of ſtone and earth. A large town had grown round it, which rendered the approach to it ſuſpicious; and the intricacy of the apartments and paſſages of the palace was ſuch, that a cautious officer would heſitate under almoſt any encouragement to enter it. I had early information that it was in effect evacuated, and I believed it; but not being certain, I did not chuſe to hazard a repulſe, nor had I force equal to any operation of doubtful ſucceſs, much leſs of enterprize. My whole ſtrength had conſiſted originally of ſix

companies

companies of Major Popham's regiment, about sixty sepoys which I had taken from the garrison of Buxar for the protection of my boats, and a few men who had been newly recruited for the Resident's guard, who had yet neither arms nor discipline. Of Major Popham's regiment eighty-two men had fallen in the massacre of Shewallah Gaut, and ninety-two were wounded. The whole number of killed and wounded of every corps and denomination, was two hundred and five. Every circumstance of an event and time so critical to the present existence and permanency of the British interests in India will merit notice in a relation of this kind. If Cheit Sing's people, after they had effected his rescue, had proceeded to my quarters at Mahdoodass's garden, instead of crouding after him in a tumultuous manner, as they did, in his passage over the river, it is most probable that my blood, and that of about thirty English gentlemen of my party, would have been added to the recent carnage; for they were above two thousand in number, furious and daring from the easy success of their last attempt: nor could I assemble more than fifty regular and armed sepoys for my whole defence. Let it not be thought that I attribute too much consequence to my own person when I suppose the fate of the British empire in India connected with it. Mean as its substance

may

may be, its accidental properties were equivalent to thofe which, like the magical characters of a Talifman in the Arabian Mythology, formed the effence of the State itfelf; reprefentation, title, and the eftimate of public opinion. Such a ftroke as that which I have fuppofed would have been univerfally confidered as decifive of the national fate: every State around it would have ftarted into arms againft it; and every fubject of its own dominion would, according to their feveral abilities, have become its enemy. What really paffed approaching to fuch an effect, from the fole apprehenfion of fuch a caufe, more than warrants the conclufion of what would have followed the caufe itfelf, had it exifted.

The effects of the firft confternation having fubfided, a number of men, reputed two thoufand, returned to Ramnagur on the 18th, under the command of Ramjeewaun, a confidential and domeftic Chief of the family.

The remainder of Major Popham's detachment, confifting of four companies of fepoys, one company of Artillery, and the company of French Rangers, lay at Mirzapore.

Thefe were ordered to march immediately to Ramnagur, Lieutenat-colonel Blair was ordered to detach a battalion of ſepoys from the garriſon of Chunar on the ſame deſtination. It was intended, that as ſoon as theſe corps had joined, and were properly equipped for ſervice, Major Popham ſhould take the command, and proceed againſt the forces quartered in Ramnagur. I wrote an order expreſs to Captain Blair, who commanded the battalion from Chunar, commanding him to halt at a ſecure diſtance from Ramnagur, and wait for further orders; and Major Popham, whom I had afterwards veſted with the command in form, wrote a ſimilar order to Captain Mayaffre, the officer commanding the reſidue of his detachment, with an additional caution to avoid hoſtilities, and attend to the ſafety of the whole party, of which, being a ſenior officer, he would have the command till Major Popham aſſumed it. To enſure the ſucceſs of his operations on that ſide, he had choſen a convenient and open plain on the ſhore oppoſite to Ramnagur for a battery of two martars, which were expected from Chunar, nor can there be a doubt, that a place ſo peculiarly ill formed for ſuch a mode of attack, and in no ſtate of defence againſt a wary aſſailant, would have proved an eaſy conqueſt. Unhappily, the ill-timed ambition of a raſh individual defeated this plan, and had nearly cauſed the deſtruction of the whole party. Captain Mayaffre unwilling, as it

appears,

appears, for no other possible motive can be ascribed to so precipitate and irregular a conduct, to lose the opportunity which his present and casual command afforded him, of acquiring a military reputation, without plan, without enquiry, against the advice of his officers, and against order, ordered the detachment to march into the narrow lanes of the town, where they were opposed by the fire of an enemy surrounding them unseen; and the party which entered were in an instant annihilated rather than defeated. Twenty-three men of the corps of Rangers, with their commander, Captain Doxat, who led the attack, were killed, and ten wounded. The first battalion of the sixth regiment of Sepoys, commanded by Captain Blair, which followed, lost fifty-seven killed, and forty-one wounded. The whole loss sustained in all the corps was, one hundred and seven killed, and seventy-two wounded. Captain Mayaffre was killed. The detachment instantly retreated. The retreat appears to have been conducted by Captain Blair, and in a manner that did him much credit. The enemy pursued with little effect, their numbers gradually lessening, till the detachment arrived within four miles of Chunar, which it regained the same evening.

This unfortunate affair happened on the morning of the 20th of August.

I confidered myfelf now as plunged in a decided war, and made every provifion both for its fpeedy termination, and its confinement to the fcene in which it had opened.

Orders were written and difpatched in multiplied copies to the different military ftations for affiftance, to the Refident of the Vizier's Court for a fupply of treafure, and to Lieutenant-colonel Blair for an inftant reinforcement. The Very few reached their deftination, the communication with every quarter being intercepted, and all the country in arms againft us; and our emiffaries, unufed to this dangerous fervice either made prifoners, or not daring to execute it, and fecreting their difpatches. Two of my letters reached Colonel Blair, who ordered Captain M'Dougal, with the fecond battalion of the fixth regiment, to march on the next day, which was the 21ft, to Benares. I now paffed an interval, like that of a dead calm preceding a violent ftorm, and fraught with all the fymptoms of its certain approach. Succeffive notices were brought to me by various channels of preparations making at Ramnagur for an affault on my quarters, which ftood in the midft of the fuburbs of Benares, and confifted of many detached buildings within one large enclofure, furrounded

rounded by houſes and trees, which intercepted every other proſpect. The whole force which I had left amounted to about four hundred and fifty men. The reports of an intended aſſault, which was fixed for that night, grew ſtronger as the day advanced. The boats on the other ſide of the river were ſeen to be in motion; and beſides the moral certainty of the real exiſtence of ſuch a deſign, the obvious advantages which it preſented to the enemy, who had nothing left to fear and nothing elſe to do, precluded all heſitation, but on the choice of expedients for defeating it. There were but two; which were, to wait the danger and try the chances of repelling it, or to retreat to a place of greater ſecurity, or of equal advantage for the encounter. The confined ſtate of the place, of which any deſcription will be inſufficient to convey an adequate idea, rendered the firſt plan impracticable. We had not a force ſufficient to guard all the defences of the place, nor a ſtore for the proviſions of a day, even for that ſmall number. The only arguments for it were, the diſgrace of a flight, and the conſideration of our wounded ſepoys, whom it might leave at the diſcretion of a mercileſs enemy. The former conſideration yielded to the ſuperior weight of neceſſity; the latter to the impoſſibility of protecting the wounded men in either caſe, as they were quartered at the diſtance

of

of near a mile from Mahoodaſs's Garden; nor would it have been poſſible in their condition, and in the multiplicity of preſſing exigencies which the reſolution to remain would have created, to remove them. Yet theſe conſiderations held me ſuſpended during the whole courſe of the day. In the evening it became neceſſary to come to a final determination, as the delay of a few hours might now preclude every option. I conſulted Major Popham. He declared the defence of the place impoſſible, and adviſed a retreat to Chunar. There were other field officers with me. I aſked for their opinions ſeparately. They clearly and unheſitatingly agreed in the ſame advice. My opinion had been determined from the inſtant I received the certain information of Captain Mayaffre's defeat. I had not yet received the news of Capt. M'Dougal's march, nor any anſwer to the letters which I had written to Lieutenant-colonel Blair for a reinforcement, nor could I know whether theſe had reached him. I yielded to the reluctance of a few minutes. My reſolution was taken and declared, and orders given to form our little corps, that we might have time to gain the open country before the enemy, having notice of the deſign, could croſs and attack us at the diſadvantage of the ſtreets, lanes, and broken ground which we had to paſs before we could reach it. Theſe orders were

iſſued

iſſued between ſeven and eight o'clock; and by eight the line was in motion, having been much retarded and impeded by an incredible tumult of ſervants, palankeens, and baggage of every denomination, which, for a time, threatened a total obſtruction to our march. Fortunately this enormous maſs took the wrong road, which left the right with a free and undiſturbed paſſage for the ſepoys. On the way we paſſed Captain McDougal's battalion about nine o'clock. We ſent him timely notice of our movement; he turned and joined us. Early the next morning we arrived at Chunar.

It is proper to mention, that as ſoon as I had formed my reſolution to leave Benares, I ſent my Moonſhy to the Nabob Saadut Ally Cawn to recommend the wounded ſepoys to his care, believing that the Rajah, from a conſideration of policy, would not chuſe to moleſt them, eſpecially as he could have no motive or object to it but revenge, if he would ſhew a determined reſolution to protect them. The ſame requeſt I made to him in writing, after my arrival at Chunar. I owe him the juſtice to atteſt, that he faithfully and liberally complied with my requeſt. He viſited them himſelf, and furniſhed them with proviſions and with money, and appointed native ſurgeons to attend them; and, as they

were

were able to bear it, he caused them all to be removed to his own quarters.

Many reports and suspicions have prevailed of his being concerned in some of the designs which were formed against us. I can neither credit nor refute them. The evil imputed to him is at best doubtful. The good which he did is certain; and he is entitled to the entire merit of it.

I avail myself of this repose in my narrative to relate another instance of private merit in Beneram Pundit, the Vakeel or Minister of the Rajah of Berar, and his brother Bissumber Pundit. These persons had come to pay their customary attendance at my quarters about the time that the line was already on the march. They immediately joined it. Some time after I saw and spoke to them, expressing some concern to find them in that situation. They were on foot without a single servant or attendant. I suffered them to accompany me till we came to the plain and halted. I then thanked them for the proof which they had shewn of their attachment, with which I was satisfied, and desired them to return, as they had a large family in Benares, which would be exposed by their continuance with me to the resentment of Cheit Sing, and perhaps to the worst effects of it; nor could

could they by their presence afford me any service which could repay what I myself should feel of compunction for suffering them to be exposed to such hazards. They refused me in a peremptory manner, without compliment, or the ostentation of performing meritorious service, and persisted, although I as peremtorily insisted on their return. I then desired that the elder brother, who was corpulent and of a constitution less equal to fatigue, would return, and the youngest only remain; but could not prevail.' A few days after my arrival at Chunar, I casually mentioned to them my distress for provisions, which was occasioned principally by the want of money; for such was our total loss of credit, that we could not raise a sufficiency even for the ordinary wants of our small detachment; and it was with great difficulty, and a degree of violence, that Lieutenant-colonel Blair extorted from the Shroffs of Chunar, who had lived and grown opulent under the protection of the garrison, the small sum of two thousand five hundred rupees, which was distributed among all the sepoys, and afforded a satisfactory relief. Beneram Pundit immediately, and with an eagerness which belonged to his character, told me, that he had a lack of rupees, in ready money, lying in his house at Benares, which I might take, if I could find any means to receive and convey it to Chunar; and the youngeſt brother adviſed, as the ſimpleſt expedient, to ſend a battalion of ſepoys for that purpoſe, which could eaſily go and return without interruption, as there were no troops ſtationed near the town on that ſide of the river, offering to accompany it himſelf, and to bring away the money. I rejected this propoſal for an obvious reaſon, and preferred the trial of the means which the Shroffs are ſuppoſed to practice for the conveyance of money on ſuch occaſions. I accepted a draught on their family for the ſum, payable to Contoo Bauboo, my Dewan, who had been left in Benares, and ſent it encloſed in a letter to him, with directions to concert with Gopaul Doſs the means of conveying it to Chunar. This proved ineffectual; Contoo Bauboo could not be found, Gopaul Doſs was ſeized (I forget at what exact period of time) and ſent a priſoner to Lutteefpoor, and in a ſhort time after Contoo Bauboo was alſo ſecured and conveyed to the ſame place of confinement. I was obliged therefore to wait for a more favourable opportunity, which never happened while I remained at Chunar. After my return to Benares, Beneram again repeated the offer, I accepted it, and received the whole amount on the inſtant, giving him a note in the Company's name, and in the uſual form for the ſame.

Examples

Examples of fidelity and national attachment merit the first reward of being recorded. In me, it is a duty, both of public and private obligation, to relate what I have related. Their merit is national, for under whatever impressions their assistance was offered, its object was the national service; nor can my person, in such an instance, be separated from my public character.

On the 20th or 21st, I forget which, I received a letter from Rajah Cheit Sing, filled with expressions of slight concern for what had passed, and professions, but indefinite and unapplied, of fidelity. I did not think it becoming to make any reply to it, and I think I ordered the bearer of the letter to be told that it required none.

On the morning of the 21st, a person came to Mr. Richard Johnson, who was one of my party, and desired his interposition with me to receive a letter and messenger from the Rajah in the evening, with proposals for an accommodation. The like application was made by Mirza Abdoola Beg, the Rajah's Vakeel, to my Dewan Contoo Bauboo, and with my permission Contoo Bauboo returned to his own house in the evening to meet the Vakeel by appointment for that purpose, by which means he missed the opportunity of going off with me, the intelligence of my intention reaching him too late for him to join me, or his infirm ſtate of body not admitting of his taking ſo haſty a reſolution. The ſubſtance of the meſſage, as it has been ſince delivered to me by Abdoola Beg in writing, was to exculpate himſelf from any concern in what had paſſed, which he charged to the inſolent behaviour of a ſervant of the Reſident, who was preſent, and the reſentment of his own people, and to profeſs his obedience and ſubmiſſion to my will in whatever way I ſhould dictate.

I regarded this as an artifice to gain time, ſince the meſſage, whatever were the ſubſtance of it, might as eaſily have been delivered in the morning as in the evening, and the meſſenger might have obtained an eaſy acceſs to me without the intrigue and myſtery of ſecret and indirect applications.

I have been ſince confirmed in this opinion by the two following anecdotes, and their exact coincidence with the deſign to which I attribute that juſt recited.

On the morning of the 21ſt, while preparations were making to croſs Capt. M'Dougal's battalion, three men, two ſtrangers, and all volunteers, went ſucceſſively to Col. Blair with intel-

ligence

ligence that a deſign was formed to eſcalade the fort of Chunar with a numerous force on that night, and an earneſt caution that he ſhould not diminiſh the ſtrength of his garriſon.

The intelligence and advice delivered by each were expreſſed nearly in the ſame words. When Captain M'Dougal's battalion was on the road, three men, ſtrangers and volunteers like the former, came to him ſucceſſively with intelligence that a large body of armed men lay in wait to intercept him at a village called Beetaburr, and warned him not to proceed. He proceeded, but did not meet a man. Lieut. Col. Blair cauſed a more than ordinary watch to be kept on that night in the fort, but not a man appeared to attack it. Not one of theſe emiſſaries has ever been ſeen ſince.

As it had been my original intention to make but a ſhort ſtay at Benares, the Nabob Vizier, in the expectation of my viſit, had already left his capital, and advanced to a ſhort diſtance to meet me. I conſidered that his preſence would prove of much ſervice by its influence on our credit, and his troops, rabble as they were, might ſerve to keep the country in awe, and to divide the attention of the enemy. But theſe advantages would invert the relation of our alliance, and give him a ſuperiority in our meeting, which would defeat

defeat the purpoſes of it; beſides that, I did not think it conſiſtent with the dignity of our government to employ a foreign aid for the ſuppreſſion of a rebellion of its own ſubjects. I therefore wrote a letter to the Nabob, requeſting him to return to Lucknow, and remain there until I ſhould have leiſure from the actual diſturbances to proſecute my original journey. The Nabob refuſed to comply with this injunction, and on the firſt intimation of my difficulties reſolved to join me; and he executed this purpoſe with ſuch apparent earneſtneſs, that he made his firſt ſtages with no other attendance than about 100 horſe, and about four companies of his body guard, with his uſual domeſtic attendants. As ſoon as I was informed of this, to remove any unfavourable impreſſion of my former letter under the conſtruction of diſtruſt, I wrote another to the Nabob, expreſſing the warmeſt ſenſe of ſuch a teſtimony of his attention, apologizing for what I had before written from an unwillingneſs to involve him in a ſcene of trouble, and expreſſing my deſire to ſee him at Chunar, according to his own wiſhes.

In the mean time I had received ſeveral intimations imputing evil deſigns to the Nabob, and warning me to guard myſelf againſt them, and eſpecially to be careful that I did not expoſe myſelf to the effects of concealed treachery, by viſiting him

him without a ſtrong guard. Many circumſtances favoured this ſuſpicion. No ſooner had the rebellion of this Zemidarry manifeſted itſelf, than its contagion inſtantly flew to Fyzabad, and the extenſive territory lying on the North of the River Dewa, and known by the names of Gooruckpoor, and Bareech. In the city of Fyzabad, Nawaub Allea and Junaaby Allea, the mother and grandmother of the Nabob, openly eſpouſed the party of Cheit Sing, encouraging and inviting people to liſt for his ſervice, and their ſervants took up arms againſt the Engliſh. Two battalions of regular ſepoys in the Vizier's ſervice, under the command of Lieut. Col. Hannay, who had been entruſted with the charge of that diſtrict, were attacked and ſurrounded in various places, many of them cut to pieces, and Col. Hannay himſelf, encompaſſed by multitudes, narrowly eſcaped the ſame fate. The Nabob Vizier was charged with being privy to the intrigues which had produced and fomented theſe diſturbances; and the little account that he ſeemed to make of them ſerved to countenance the ſuſpicion. I can truly ſay for myſelf, that I never afforded it the ſlighteſt degree of credit: neither his character, the tenor of his paſt conduct, the expectations which I knew he entertained of aſſiſtance and relief from myſelf, nor his inability to ſupport himſelf without the protection of our government, allowing me for a

moment

moment to entertain a thought ſo injurious to his fidelity, and ſo contrary to probability; yet I was not perfectly free from apprehenſions ſimilar to ſuch a ſuggeſtion. The Nabob was ſurrounded by men baſe in their characters, and improvident in their underſtandings, his favourites and the companions of his looſer hours. Theſe had every cauſe to dread the effect of my influence on theirs; and both theſe, and the relations of the family, whoſe views of conſequence and power were intercepted by our participation in the adminiſtration of his affairs, entertained a mortal hatred to our nation, and openly avowed it. Theſe all joined in preſcribing the moſt pernicious and fatal counſels to the Nabob, repreſenting this as the time to deliver himſelf from what they deſcribed as the yoke of ſervitude. Although he firmly rejected all their perſuaſions, and I was aſſured of it, yet he himſelf was at their mercy, and it was in their power to uſe both his authority and his perſon for the perpetration of their own deſigns; nor could I uſe any precaution to avoid them, which would not appear to proceed from a diſtruſt of the Nabob himſelf. I never communicated my apprehenſions, nor acted from them, and had the ſatisfaction of receiving the Nabob, of maintaining an intercourſe with him, with every mark of the moſt ſecure and mutual confidence; and of parting

parting with him with every demonſtration of mutual ſatisfaction.

I had before written to Col. Morgan for aſſiſtance. I now repeated the order; and as the iſſue of a war, begun with ſuch diſadvantages on our ſide, and with the total loſs of the country, was doubtful, I added an order to follow with his whole force, with another to Col. Sir John Cumming who commanded at Futtehgur, to ſupply his place at Cawnpoor. I conſidered that if we were ſucceſsful with a leſs exertion, it would be eaſy to countermand theſe orders before the troops could have advanced far in the execution of them; but if we failed of ſucceſs, and ſuch orders were not ſent, it might be too late to iſſue them with any hope of effect from them, or even of their being received; ſince the communication, which was now very difficult and uncertain, might then be abſolutely precluded. None of my letters reached Col. Morgan till he had taken his reſolution. Reports were conveyed to him of my ſituation and paſt miſadventures. The ſudden failure of intelligence convinced him of the truth of what he heard; and juſtly concluding that orders had been ſent which had been ſtopped in their way to him, he at once reſolved to execute their ſuppoſed and obvious purport, and detached a force ſuperior to that which I had required to my aſſiſtance. It conſiſted of two regiments of ſepoys, thirty European artillery men, and two companies of the European regiments, with four ſix pounders, one howitz, tumbrils, ammunition, draft and carriage cattle. For the greater expedition, he ordered this detachment to proceed by water. The zeal of the officers, ſo well ſeconded that of their commander, that although it appears that the Reſolution was taken on the 29th, the whole were embarked, and in *movement*, on the 31ſt of the month. Major Crabb commanded the detachment.

A long interval of time, which acquired its full meaſure, from the magnitude of the events which were expected to grow out of it, and their uncertain production, paſſed in total ignorance of the ſucceſs of the various orders which had been diſpatched, and of the ſuccours which might be preparing for us. One-half of the province of Owd, was in a ſtate of as complete rebellion as that of Benares. Hutteh Shaw had invaded Sircar Sârun, in our own province, of Bahar, ſupported by ſupplies of money, and encouraged with promiſes of more from Cheit Sing: Many of the Zemindars of Bahar, had diſcovered ſymptoms of diſaffection; and reports were made to me of levies of men openly entertained for the enemy, from our ſubjects in that province. Even

the

the wretched ſubjects of Napal, dared to ſeize, by force, ſome villages, to which they had a claim, and had ſometime before ſupplicated the attention of our government towards it. In my impatience for advices, I dreaded that every packet would bring a freſh accumulation to our diſtreſſes, and the news of commotion in every quarter. At this period, a letter found its way to me from Colonel Muir, who commanded the army employed againſt Madajee Sindia, informing me of overtures made by that chief for a ſeparate peace. This had been one of the objects of my journey to this quarter; but eagerly as I had ſought ſuch an event, I was proportionably mortified to learn with what facility it might have been accompliſhed, and how unſeaſonably our domeſtic misfortunes had happened to defeat ſo fair a proſpect of it. I had no money or credit, equal to the ſupply of 3000 rupees; and by an unfortunate train of official perplexities, which had happened ſome time preceding this, both Major Popham's regiment, the Rangers, and all the corps of the garriſon of Chunar, were four months in *arrears*. This was our ſituation.

What force could be ſpared from the garriſon of Chunar, added to Major Popham's regiment, was formed into a detachment under his command, and encamped on a plain about a mile to the eastward of Chunar. The greatest strength of the enemy was collected at Pateeta, about seven miles from Chunar, in the same direction.

On the 27th of August, Lieutenant Polhill arrived with six companies of sepoys belonging to the Nabob Vizer's body guard, stationed at Allahabad. He was ordered to encamp on the opposite bank of the river, for the purpose of keeping our communication open with the shore. On the 29th, he attacked and defeated a considerable body of troops, under the command of a principal chief, named Shaub Cawn, who was stationed at a small fort and town, called Seeker, within sight of Chunar. The advantages gained by this success were the removal of that part of enemy, and the acquisition of a considerable booty in grain, which had been the object of the enterprize.

On the 3d of September, Major Popham detached Captain Blair, with his battalion, and two companies of his own grenadiers, to surprize the camp at Pateeta. They marched at three in the morning, and arrived at the ground by daylight, but found it abandoned, and the enemy waiting for them in complete order, at about a mile beyond it. A bloody action ensued, in which the enemy, as might be expected from

men

men flushed with recent successes, fought with a desperate intrepidity. Our sepoys began to break into disorder, when by a well-timed and successful attack of the enemy's guns by the two companies of grenadiers, headed by Lieutenants Fallon and Birrell, the fortune of the day turned in our favour, and the field was left in our possession, with four guns and four tumbrils. One of the guns, its carriage being broken, was spiked and left. The other three, with one of the tumbrils, loaded with as much ammunition as it could carry, were brought away. The other three tumbrils, with two hundred maunds of loose powder, were blown up. About 1500 round shot of different weight, and mostly hammered, were found, and left in a village adjacent.

Our loss in the action, was very great: We had 48 men killed, and 85 wounded. That of the enemy was unknown, but must have been considerable. Their guns were well served, and it was from their execution that we principally suffered. It was remarkable that they had all the apparatus of our artillery, such as port fires, tubes, chain and quilted grape shot, &c. equal, or nearly equal, to the production of an European laboratory. Samples of each kind will be sent to the Board. Their artillery did

not

not anſwer to the quailty of the ſtores. One gun was of modern caſt, and with its carriage, which was not bad, ſaid to have been made at Ramnagur. The others were of a very old caſt and conſtruction, and their carriages bad and much worn. This was the general character of all the ordnance taken in the courſe of the war.

Dearly as this victory was purchaſed, with the expenditure of one-fourth of the party, it was yet a victory, aſcertained and acknowledged, and had its due effect of impreſſing the enemy with diſcouragement, and our own men with confidence; and it was an earneſt of our future ſucceſs in the public opinion, which is, at all times, of high importance to our political influence, and was eſpecially ſo at this, in which the minds of all men were ſuſpended, for the deciſion of the part which they were to take, either in the immediate conteſt, or in their own conduct as dependent on it.

I muſt not omit in this place, an inſtance of vengeance which marks the ſanguinary character of Cheit Sing, and too ſtrongly proves, that if the other exceſſes committed by his people, were not authorized by his expreſs order, they

were

were perpetrated under the influence of his example, and the knowledge of his inclination.

Fourteen men of the corps of Rangers, had been left ſick at Mirzapoor, when the remainder of Major Popham's detachment marched under the command of Captain Mayaffre to Ramnagur. They were made priſoners and ſent to Lutteeſpoor. They arrived there on the 3d of September, about the ſame time that news was received of Captain Blair's action at Pateeta, which happened on that morning. What provocation they gave, or whether any, is not known. It is ſurmiſed, but I know not the authority, that one of theſe unhappy men expreſſed a joy on hearing that our arms had been ſucceſsful. They were all butchered on the ſpot, and almoſt in the immediate preſence of the Rajah, except one man, who made a ſhift to crawl with a mangled body to the neighbouring woods, where he ſubſiſted for a few days; returned to the fort, received mercy, and is ſtill living and in our camp. The particulars of this maſſacre have been ſince verified with ſome uneſſential variations from my relation of it, in an affidavit of the ſurvivor, which will be annexed.

On

On the 10th of September, at about ſeven in the morning, Major Crabb's detachment appeared on the oppoſite ſhore. It conſiſted of the corps already related. It had proceeded as far as Illahabad by water, but been much retarded in its courſe by ſtrong and adverſe winds; on which account, the courſe of the river alſo winding very much between Illahabad and Chunar, Major Crabb had prudently diſembarked the men and ſtores, and marched them by the high road, remanding the boats to Cawnpoor, whither, indeed, their return would have been impracticable, had they paſſed the boundary of this Zemidarry.

Major Roberts, with his regiment, and a lack of rupees in ſilver, arrived on the 13th of September from Lucknow, to which place, as I have before related, he had been ordered to repair for the guard of my perſon, in my intended viſit to that capital. A further ſupply of fifty thouſand rupees was a few days after received from the Nabob's Aumil of Illahabad.

The money was immediately diſtributed among all the troops in equal proportions; and by ſatisfying their wants, facilitated Major Popham's preparatives for the commencement of active operations.

I have

I have a pleaſure in teſtifying that, diſtreſſed as the ſepoys had been for the want of money, they had never manifeſted the leaſt ſymptom of diſcontent. I had frequently viſited the camp, and paſſed the lines each time in review. Once, and only once, I heard one or two voices of complaint, but neither clamorous nor diſreſpectful.

On the 11th, the Nabob Vizier arrived at his encampment, which had been formed on the oppoſite ſhore. I choſe to make him the firſt viſit, which was performed on the ſame morning, and was returned by him on the next.

Hyder Beg, the Nabob's ſecond Miniſter, arrived at the ſame time. He had been deputed early to meet me at Benares, and had arrived there about two days after my departure from it. Inſtead of following me to Chunar, he had ſuffered himſelf to be detained by Lalla Bucherauge, the Shroff, who had promiſed to accompany him with a ſupply of money. In the mean time, a ſudden and great ſwell of the river rendered the Burna Nulla, behind which he was encamped, impaſſable. The Rajah's people, at the ſame time, carried away all the boats; and after a long and fruitleſs negotiation with them for an unmoleſted paſſage, which he did not think it prudent to attempt at the hazard of an oppoſition, he

 at

at length did attempt it, and met none. His indecision on this occasion, furnished ground for various suppositions; but I knew, and had assurances from a person in my suite, who had taken refuge with him and acquired his confidence, and on whose authority I could implicitly rely, that they were wholly devoid of foundation. I had a pleasing and incontrovertible evidence of his fidelity, soon after the conclusion of our troubles, in a letter which Captain Blair picked up at Lutteefpoor, and which I shall add to the appendix; not merely as a justification of that Minister, but as a relief to the dry and unentertaining materials with which it is associated, if it shall convey the same opinion of the good sense of the writer to other minds, as it has done to mine.

On the 15th, Lieutenant Polhil crossed and joined Major Popham's camp. The whole detachment now consisted of the following strength, viz.

1 company of European grenadiers, commanded by Captain Grant.

1	ditto	ditto	light infantry	ditto	Capt. Harrison.
1	ditto	French Rangers		ditto	Lieut. Wade.
30	European artillery men			ditto	Capt. Hill.
1	regiment of sepoys		the 7th	ditto	Major Crabb.
1	ditto	- - - - - -	19th	ditto	Major Balfour.
1	ditto	- - - - - -	30th	ditto	Major Roberts.
1	ditto	- - - - - -	35th	ditto	Major Popham.
1	battalion, the 1st of the 6th regiment			ditto	Captain Blair.
6	companies of the Nabob's body guards			ditto	Lieut. Polhill

The

The following is a catalogue of Cheit Sing's whole force, which has been ſince delivered to me by one of his principal officers; and as it made a part of the affidavit, I admit it and credit it as genuine. It is certainly not exagerated.

LIST of the eſtabliſhed forces in the ſervice of Cheit Sing, Cavalry, Sepoys, Matchlock men, &c. &c.

Cavalry — — — —	1700
Select troops or body guards, horſe and foot	700
Sepoys — — — — —	1150
Matchlock men — — — —	1800
Attached to Bullum Daſs, horſe 300, foot 500	800
With Shujan Sing, cavalry and infantry, 500 with two guns, Sepoys and artillery men, 340	840
With Munnear Sing, cavalry and infantry —	700
Total eſtabliſhed troops ——	7690

Troops entertained after the arrival of Cheit Sing, at Luteeſpore

Firſt, entertained at Luteeſpore, Matchlock and Sword men — — — —	2000
Second, Nujjeeb Sword men, from Lucknow	1000
Total ——	3000

Troops aſſembled from different places, horſe and foot, with Jugger Deave Sing — —	500
Matchlock men arrived with Bukht Sing, by order, from the Rajah — —	1200
With Gomaun Sing, ſent for by the Rajah, Matchlock men — — —	500
From the Fowjdar of Biddevi arrived, Matchlock men — — —	1000
Raje Poots, of the tribe of Rugbunſe, from Kurraukut — — —	3000

Arrived with Dullun Sing, Foujdar of Mukurun, Badſhahpoor Matchlocks — —	1500
Cavalry and infantry, arrived with Ruzza Cooli Khan from Mirzapoor — —	300
Rajepoots collected from Agoree and Purwah, by Dia Lutchoo — —	500
Of the tribe or caſt of Kammaur, collected by Shujan Sing — — —	1000
Sword and Matchlock men with Ramjeewawm	2000
Total troops in the ſervice of Cheit Sing ——	22190

To which are to be added huſbandmen and adventurers, who took up arms voluntarily, making the foregoing number amount to near forty thouſand.

Theſe forces were divided between Lutteefpoor, Pateetah, and Ramnagur. The beſt reputed of them were at Pateetah, and the great Maſs compoſing the laſt corps, with a part of the others, at Lutteefpoor with the Rajah, who had fixed his reſidence at that place ſince his flight from Shewallah Gaut.

Before I proceed, it may not be improper to ſtate the reſource on which he, not very unreaſonably, depended for lengthening the war, if not for ſucceſs in the courſe of it.

First, his fortreſſes; of which there are many, and ſome of conſiderable extent and ſtrength, erected in various parts of the Zemidarry. Of

theſe

theſe the two principal are Bidjeygur and Luteefpoor. Ramnagur ſcarcely deſerves to be named with them, and Pateetah has been rendered conſiderable, only by its having heen a capital ſcene of oppoſition and of our victories.

Bidjeygur is a fort erected on the ſolid rock, of a hill riſing to the height of 745 perpendicular feet from the level ground. It lies about fifty miles in a ſouth-eaſt direction from Chunar. It was the depoſitory of all his and his father's treaſures.

Luteefpoor is a large fort built with ſtone, and ſurrounded by hills, and either from neglect or deſign, obſtructed from diſtant view by trees and thick ſhrubs ſurrounding it. It lies about 14 miles eaſtward from Chunar.

Pateetah is a very large town, ſurrounded by a rampart of earth, extending to a great diſtance beyond it to the hills adjoining. The fort itſelf is a ſmall ſquare houſe of ſtone, itſelf fortified with four round towers, and encloſed with a high rampart, and a ditch, which is in moſt parts broad and deep. Its greateſt advantage againſt an enemy, to whom delay was defeat, was, that it was inviſible to its aſſiailants.

Ramnagur has been deſcribed already. The other forts, whatever their conſequence under a different

different train of ſucceſſes might have been, are of none to the events of this narrative.

His next great reſource was his wealth, on which he looked, and thought himſelf invincible, an expreſſion which I borrow from one of the meanneſt of his dependants. It is credibly affirmed, that he inherited from his father, Bulwant Sing, a complete crore of rupees, to which it is believed that he made conſiderable additions.

The diſtreſſes of our government, and the power and number of its enemies, may alſo be reckoned, though negative, yet amongſt his reſources. The reſt were deluſory, which the falſe and violent counſels of his brother, Shujan Sing, and his buxey Saddanund, impoſed on his inexperience, and the pliancy and aptitude of his diſpoſition.

It would break the attention, and perplex the thread of the narrative, to relate every diſtinct event in its exact order of time. I have therefore in the minuter points, endeavoured rather to arrange them according to their relation to the greater, or to find a place for them in the vacant intervals and pauſes of it. It may be proper in this place to mention, that during the time of inaction, which ſucceded to my arrival at Chunar, I received ſeveral letters from Cheit Sing, beſides

letters

letters from Mr. Barnet, and one from Contoo Baboo, who were both his prisoners at Luteefpoor, which were written by his order. These were all alike in substance, containing acknowledgments and professions of his submission to my authority, assertions of his own innocence, charging the massacre of Shewallah to the Chobdar, whose insults provoked the resentment of his servants, whom he could not restrain; and claim a merit from his having in the three past actions been the suffering part, though successful, and in none the aggressor; adding general offers of accommodation, and in the letters written by his order, a pompous display of his inexhaustible wealth, the multitude and bravery of his forces, and the devoted affection and fidelity of all his subjects. I refused to answer them, letting him know that they were written with too much presumption, in the style of equality, and with inapplicable professions, which were no better than none. Some of these letters will appear in the appendix. The rest were lost.

It had been intended to begin our operations with the attack of Ramnagur; partly because it had been the scene of our first disgrace, and principally because the repossession of the capital, which would follow the capture of Ramnagur, would, it was thought, redeem our credit with the public, and be deemed equivalent in the distant

diſtant reports of it, to the complete recovery of our authority over the country; as the exiſtence of a fugitive chief in the wilds and mountains would be little regarded, when he was expelled from the capital of his government, and the ſeat of his collections. For this purpoſe, battering cannon and mortars were ordered to Major Popham's camp, and every other preparative made for a ſiege. This cauſed the delay of ſome days. In the mean time, a man named Bundoo Cawn, a native and inhabitant of the town of Chunar, gave information that, as the Rajah's force was principally collected at Lutteefpoor and Pateetah, and was daily accumulating, it would become exceedingly difficult to diſlodge him, if he was allowed to gain too great ſtrength there, by a proceſs of detailed and conſecutive operations; that the approaches both to Pateetah and Luteefpoor were ſtrongly guarded, and eſpecially thoſe of Luteefpoor, which he deſcribed as unaſſailable, but with a great and certain loſs, on this ſide, the only road to it lying through Pateetah; and even if carried, untenable from the ſtrength of the paſs behind it, of which the enemy would keep poſſeſſion in defiance of all our efforts, and againſt any ſuperiority of numbers. This paſs takes its name from the adjacent village of Suckroot. He adviſed a divided plan of attack to be executed at the ſame point of time; one on the fort of Pateetah, the

other

other on the paſs of Suckroot; of which our forces coming on it by ſurprize, it being unguarded and eaſier of acceſs from above, might eaſily obtain poſſeſſion, and by that means gain the ſame advantage over the garriſon of Luteefpoor, as that would have over us, if we firſt took poſſeſſion of the fort; with the command of every road of communication, if, which he did not doubt, we ſucceeded againſt Pateetah. He offered to conduct the party which ſhould be deſtined on the ſervice againſt the paſs of Suckroot, by a road unfrequented and unknown, which he deſcribed with a minute, and, as it has ſince appeared, correct detail. The confidence with which he ſpoke, and the conſiſtency of his aſſertions and reaſonings upon them, acquired a great additional ſtrength from his former recent conduct. He had accompanied Captain Blair in both actions of Ramnagur and Pateeta, and had been very ſerviceable to that officer by his knowledge of the ground, and by his advice in the application of it. His ſervice on both occaſions had been gratuitous, nor did he profeſs any motive for that which he now offered, but the intereſt and ſafety of a large family which depended on our ſucceſs.

Major Popham at once ſaw the propriety of his advice, and adopted it. The evening of the

15th, was appointed for the first execution of the plan. In the mean time, it was concealed with the most profound secrecy. As a security for the fidelity and steadiness of Bundoo Cawn, he had a promise of a jagheer in perpetuity for himself and family, if the enterprize succeeded. This engagement has been since amply performed. Major Popham formed his army into two divisions, one destined for the more distant enterprize, and commanded by Major Crabb. It consisted of the 7th regiment, Major Crabb's; the 1st battalion of the 6th regiment; Lieutenant Polhill's six companies of the Nabob's body guard; four six-pounders, and a five and half-inch howitz. These corps were told off, and began their march about eleven that night. Major Popham began his march with the other division at about three o'clock in the morning to Pateetah.

On his arrival there he found the works much stronger, and the approach more hazardous, than he had expected from the description which had been given of the place. He applied for the two battering cannon and the mortars which had been originally intended for the attack of Ramnagur, and remanded on the change of the plan. They were sent, but made no impression; and he resolved, on the encouragement of of a five days experience, and from the fear of a delay operating againſt the other part of his plan, to attempt a ſtorm. This was ordered and executed on the morning of the 20th, with an inſtant and compleat ſucceſs. Major Roberts commanded the ſtorming party. The enemy made a ſlight ſtand at the outer entrenchment, and fled through the fort, our men following without oppoſition. A ſlight attack was made at this time on our camp, but repelled with ſome loſs on the part of the enemy, and none on ours. We loſt during the ſiege eleven men killed, beſides ten wounded.

On the ſame morning, Major Crabb having conducted his diviſion through almoſt impracticable ways, arrived at a village called Lora, which lies about two miles from the paſs. Here he found a body of men with three guns poſted to oppoſe him. They made a firm ſtand, but were defeated with a conſiderable loſs.—Ours was twelve men of every denomination killed, and twenty-two wounded. The enemy fled through the paſs to Lutteefpoor. Our detachment followed to the head of the paſs, and there encamped for the remainder of the day.

The news of theſe concurrent ſucceſſes being conveyed to the Rajah, at the ſame inſtant of

 time,

time, alarmed him exceedingly for his own perſonal ſafety. His fears were excited with a more forcible impreſſion by the ſurpriſe of the advance of ſo great a force from a quarter where he had not expected any. With his face turned towards Chunar, and his whole attention and that of his people directed to the movements which were made on that ſide, they had no ſuſpicion of any deſign being formed behind them. The firſt intelligence which was received of Major Crabb's party, deſcribed it as conſiſting of the followers of Ooſſaun Sing, and only three companies of our Sepoys; the Hircarrahs who conveyed the news, poſſibly miſtaking the advanced guard for the whole force, and reporting it accordingly; nor was the real ſtrength of the party known, even by that which was detached to oppoſe it, until the inſtant of the action. This circumſtance was related at the time, and has been ſince confirmed to me by an officer, named Myher, who commanded a ſmall body of the Rajah's ſepoys, and the guns in the action. No deſign could be more judiciouſly planned, or more happily executed. Even the impediments and diſappointments which attended it, ſerved but to promote the coincidence of the final movements of its operation, with ſo well-timed an effect, that the difference of time which paſſed between the engagement at Lora and the conqueſt of Pateetah, was little

little more than that which would be required by the difference of the diſtances of each from Lutteefpoor, for the news of each ſucceſs to reach Lutteefpoor at the ſame inſtant.

Cheit Sing inſtantly prepared for flight. His road to Bidjeygur, which was his laſt refuge, lay through the paſs, which he durſt not attempt. He left Lutteefpoor about three or four in the afternoon; and making a circuit over the hills, gained the high road at the diſtance of ſome miles beyond the paſs, and proceeded with a few followers to the neighbourhood of Bidjeygur. Some others followed and rejoined him. The reſt left without orders, ſtayed but to plunder the place, and evacuated it. The Gawng Wallahs, or militia, compoſed of the huſbandmen, who had been ſummoned to attend him, all fled to their own homes. So rapid was the report of this event in its communication, and ſo deciſive in its effects, that the fort of Sutteeſſgur, which lies about ſeven or eight miles to the northward of Lutteefpoor, and the palace of Ramnagur, were evacuated on the ſame evening; and the allegiance of the whole country reſtored as completely in the courſe of a few hours, from a ſtate of univerſal revolt, to its proper channel, as if it had never departed from it.

On

On the next morning, the 21st, Major Crabb marched through the paſs to Luteefpoor, and found it abandoned.

On the ſame day, Major Moſes Crawford, with the 28th regiment of Sepoys, arrived from Dinapoor, and joined the detachment.

Major Balfour was detached on the morning of the 22d to Ramnagur, of which he took quiet poſſeſſion. No one remained to oppoſe him.

Being deſirous of returning without loſs of time to Benares, and the preſence of the Nabob Vizier being more urgently required for the quiet of his country, we parted on the 25th, with every expreſſion of mutual and real ſatisfaction.

On the next morning I arrived at Ramnagur, and on the 28th returned to my old quarters at Mahdoodaſs's Garden at Benares.

To quiet the minds of the people, proclamations were iſſued, offering pardon to all who ſhould peaceably return to their obedience, excepting the perſons of Cheit Sing, and his brother

ther Shujan Sing, whom their late rebellious conduct, and their rancour manifested to our nation in the deliberate murder of our soldiers, and even defenceless passengers, who had the misfortue to fall into their hands, had precluded from every title to lenity. Among the unhappy sufferers to whom the above exception alluded, was a person of the name of Hooker, who had followed the occupation of a dealer in European wares to our camps, and had ventured to pass in his budgerow, a little after the unhappy affair of Shewallah, near Ramnagur, where he was seized, and unarmed as he was, and pleading the innocence of his profession, murdered in cold blood, Shujan Sing had the command at that time in Ramnagur. Two soldiers also, of Major Crabb's detachment, having wandered from the line, were taken and murdered at Gopee Gunge. For this reason that town was excepted in the proclamation, and has since been destroyed.

My first care, after my return to Benares, was to determine the succession to the Zemidarry and Rauge, vacated by the forfeiture of Cheit Sing. The right of the Company to the disposal of it certainly had not suffered by the past events. The territory had been wholly lost to their dominion, and wholly conquered by their arms: yet the rest

of

of the family, who formerly possessed it, had not merited by any act of theirs, to be involved in the punishment of a man who had been equally their enemy, and whom they had regarded as the usurper of their more legal rights; nor perhaps, would it have been prudent to have put the submission of the people to the test of a new species of dominion. I therefore resolved, in virtue of the full powers which I possessed from the Board for that purpose, to bestow it on the next lineal heir. This was Bauboo Mehipnarain. He was the grandson of Rajah Bulwunt Sing, by a daughter married to Bauboo Doorgbijey Sing. The widow of Bulwunt Sing, named Ranny Goolaub Koower, was still living and in an extreme old age. By the Hindoo law she might claim the inheritance. Her daughter also, the wife of Doorgbijey Sing, might assert the like pretension. Had it become a matter of contest, I had resolved to leave it to the decision of the whole body of the Pundits of Benares; but this reference was unnecessary. Doorgbijey Sing yielded up the pretension of his wife, and the old Ranny her own, by a writing sealed with her name, and acknowledged in the presence of a confidential person whom I deputed to her for that purpose, declaring it to be her wish and request, that the Rauje might be conferred on her grandson, Mehipnarain. He was accordingly invested and proclaimed on the

the 30th of September. His father, Bauboo Doorgbijey Sing, was at the ſame time inveſted with the office of Naib, and is in effect the ſole acting manager. He is about thirty-five years of age, his ſon nineteen.

I have thought it proper to eſtabliſh a diſtinct and independent magiſtracy for the town of Benares. Allee Ibrahim Cawn, the perſon choſen for this charge, was duly in veſted with it on the 29th of October.

On the 5th of November I concluded the ſettlement of the revenue which was to be paid by Rajah Mehipnarain, being 33,33,33358 for the current year, and a perpetual rent of 40,00,000 rupees for the future.

It has been already mentioned, that ſoon after my flight to Chunar, Colonel Muir adviſed me of overtures made by Mahdajee Sindia for a ſeparate peace. I ſent to Colonel Muir credentials and inſtructions; and on the 13th of October a treaty was concluded with Mahdajee Sindia. To confirm and improve the advantages obtained by it, I deputed Mr. Anderſon to Mahdajee Sindia, and at the ſame time ſent Mr. Chapman, with Biſſumber Pundit on a ſimilar commiſſion to Moodajee Booſla, the Rajah of Berar.

On the 8th of October, Major Naylor, with the 23d regiment, having been detached to the relief of Lieutenant-colonel Hannay, arrived on the northern banks of the Dewar, defeated a large force which had aſſembled round Colonel Hannay, and entirely diſperſed them. The return of the Nabob ſoon after effectually reſtored the quiet of the country.

About the ſame time a regiment of ſepoys, under the command of Major Lucas, defeated and drove Futty Shaw from the diſtrict of Sircar Saurun.

After having gained poſſeſſion of Lutteefpoor, Major Popham loſt no time in proſecuting his march to Bidjeygwe. Cheit Sing did not wait his approach, but fled, taking with him as much treaſure as his elephants and camels could carry, which has been reported to me to have conſiſted of one lack of mohrs, and fifteen or ſixteen of ſilver, beſides jewels to an unknown amount. His wife, a woman of an amiable character, his mother Pauna, and all the other women of his family, and the ſurvivors of the family of his father Bulwunt Sing, who were connected with his, were left in the fort of Bidjeygur. He took the route of Rewa, and from thence proceeded to Panna, the capital of Boondelcund, paying and plundered as he paſſed. He was by the laſt advices in that country, the Rajah profeſſing in

his

his letters to me a resolution to withdraw his protection from him, and secretly favouring him.

The fortress of Bidjeygur surrendered by capitulation on the 10th of November, yielding to Major Popham the peculiar credit of having surmounted all the obstacles which nature and art has opposed to the conquest of two of the fortresses of Hindostan, which had been before universally deemed impregnable.

I have now brought my narrative to its proper conclusion, at that point in which all the movements which form the subject of it, and all their objects appear to have attained their full and complete termination. I regret the length to which it has been drawn, and fear that it will appear unreasonable to those who may consider it a point of duty to give it a thorough perusal and who will scarce fail to reflect, that it contains in effect the history of but one month. To myself the reflection affords a different sensation when applied to the multitude of events, and their magnitude comprized within so short an interval of my public life. I have aimed at brevity, both in the selection of facts and in the narration of them; having omitted every circumstance which, though engaging a portion of my attention at the time, had no connection with the general train of events, or influence on the character by which

 they

they are discriminated from the ordinary course of affairs. For the satisfaction of such as shall have more patience or leisure to look into them, I have added as an appendix, copies of all the material papers which have a relation to the narrative, but which would have encreased the bulk of it, and disturbed the attention, if inserted in the body of it.

I have also added attestations of all the principal facts and events, sworn before the Chief Justice, to whose advice I am obliged for having suggested it. It did not strike my mind that matters of such notoriety here would require some more authentic verification of them at home than the recital of the man, whose reputation is so immediately concerned as mine is, in the judgment which my superiors, and which the public at large will have a right to form upon it. I am sensible of the wisdom of the precaution, and sorry that it was not earlier intimated, that I might have had time to have collected a larger fund of evidence, although I have reason to be satisfied with the weight of that which I have obtained. Let it be also remembered, that this relation itself has been written under the force of an obligation, as binding as that of an oath administered and taken in all its legal forms.

Whatever

Whatever judgment may be paſſed on my particular conduct, I am yet happy that it has proved the means of calling forth the inherent virtue of my countrymen, and diſplaying to all the powers and people of India both the national character and the national conſtitution, by ſuch effects as have been unrecorded in their hiſtories, and are ſcarce conceivable by their habit of thinking.

The ſuddenneſs of our calamities, the diſtance of aſſiſtance, the privation of every preſent reſource; the manifeſt intereſt which animated and impelled every corps and every individual to the ſupport of the common cauſe; and the rapidity with which they ruſhed to repel the common danger, are facts of univerſal obſervation; and will contribute more effectually to the permanency of the Britiſh influence and dominion, than the moſt ſplendid victories obtained over adverſaries of the higheſt reputation; becauſe it ſhews the harmony which unites all the parts of our government, and their augmented ſtrength under the compreſſion of external violence; and will be remembered as a moſt ſtriking example, which every man concerned in its operations will apply to his own intereſts and feelings; that its greateſt and moſt ſucceſsful exertions have ariſen out of the moſt deſperate emergencies, and have fallen in every ſuch inſtance with the moſt dreadful vengeance on the heads of its aggreſſors.

For

For the ſenſe which I have entertained of the particular conduct of the officers who have diſtinguiſhed themſelves in the late ſervice, I cannot expreſs myſelf in ſtronger terms that thoſe of the following extract of my letter to the Board, dated the 29th of September, and copy of one dated the 7th of October.

Extract of a letter from the Governor-general to the Board, dated 29th September, 1781.

" I have forborne any particular comments " in this place, reſerving them, where they " will be more properly introduced, for my " detailed narrative. Yet I cannot ſuppreſs " without a violence to my own feelings the " teſtimony which is due, eſpecially from me, " to the unexampled zeal and public ſpirit of all " our officers, and the wonderful activity with " which theſe qualities were diſplayed on the " late occaſion. I have already acknowledged " the early exertions which were made by Colonel " Blair, during my former ſhort and calami- " ous reſidence at Benares. Of Major Popham " I cannot ſay ſufficient, to expreſs my ſenſe of " his ſervices. Though my letters were every " where intercepted, Colonel Morgan, with a " deciſion and ſolicitude that reflect equal credit " upon his character, detached Major Crabb, " with his party, to my aſſiſtance on the firſt

" and

" and inſtant rumour of my ſituation. Colonel " Sir John Cumming, with the like alacrity, " obeyed the orders for his march to Cawnpoor; " as did Lieutenant Colonel Ahmuty, in the im- " mediate diſpatch of Major Crawford, and the " troops of cavalry. The ſame ſpirit animated " every officer of every corps, and infuſed itſelf " into the men under their command with an ef- " fect ſo far exceeding the common occurrences " of human affairs, that in the complete ſpace " of one month, this great and valuable Province, " which had been ſuddenly and wholly loſt, was " in ſubſtance wholly recovered to the Britiſh " empire.

" I am, &c."

Copy of a letter from the Governor-General to the Board, dated the 7th of October.

" I have had frequent occaſion to expreſs, in " public orders, the higheſt approbation of the " zeal, ſpirit, and good conduct exerted by all the " officers and troops in all the late operations for " reducing the rebellious Zemidarry to obedience. " Several of the officers have merited and receiv- " ed particular thanks by name, and it would " give me the greateſt ſatisfaction to diſtinguiſh " and reward each individual in proportion to his " ſtation and ſervices. But as no government is " poſſeſſed of the means of ſuch diffuſive re-

" compence,

"compence, it muſt be unavoidably confined to "thoſe whoſe elevated rank, or peculiar ſitua- "tion, affords them opportunities of laying im- "mediate claim to the more honorary or bene- "ficial teſtimonies of public gratitude. But "ſuch teſtimonies, whilſt they are in poſſeſſion "of perſons of ſuperior rank, give hopes to, "and excite the emulation of thoſe alſo who are "in the inferior; and thus, by well-timed and "judicious rewards, the proſperity of the ſtate "and the intereſts of its ſervants are united.

"It is on this principle that I requeſt permiſ- "ſion to ſolicit the conſideration of the Board, "for an honourable recompence to the two offi- "cers who have been firſt in rank, and moſt "conſpicuous in ſervices, during the commo- "tions in this diſtrict.

"Lieutenant-Colonel Blair, who commanded "at Chunargur, from the day of the fatal cata- "ſtrophe in this town, manifeſted a generous "zeal for the public intereſts, and for my ſafety, "above all conſiderations for his own. Every "requiſition which I made to him was inſtantly "complied with, and he ſent me a reinforcement "of a battalion of Sepoys, at a time when he "had the ſtrongeſt grounds to believe, that an "attack would be made on his own garriſon, "which it was incapable of ſuſtaining.

"It

" It is perhaps ſcarce leſs meritorious in Colo-
" nel Blair to have not only ſubmitted without
" repining to the preference of any inferior offi-
" cer to a command of ſuch importance within
" the limits of his own, but to have aſſiſted and
" co-operated with that officer with as much ala-
" cirity, as if the ſucceſs was to have redounded
" to his own honour.

" This is not the firſt occaſion on which the
" attention of the Board has been called to the
" diſtinguiſhed merit and ſervices of Major Pop-
" ham. They have been again moſt happily ex-
" erted in his preſent command for the ſafety
" and intereſts of the company in a very perilous
" ſituation. I have been in a manner eye wit-
" neſs of them. I wiſh to expreſs and to ſhew
" my ſenſe of them, but I want language for
" the firſt, and means for the latter.

" As from the knowledge which I have of the
" characters of Lieutenant-Colonel Blair and
" Major Popham, I am certain that the moſt
" honourable reward will be to them the moſt
" acceptable one. I beg leave to propoſe, that
" they be promoted by Brevet to the rank im-
" mediately above that which they at preſent re-
" ſpectively hold ; that is, Lieutenant-Colonel
" Blair to the rank of Colonel, and Major Pop-

"ham to the rank of Lieutenant-Colonel.—
"This preferment, whilst it is an honourable
"distinction to these officers, cannot be deemed
"an injury to their seniors; as their promotion
"will not be thereby retarded: They may be al-
"ways employed on separate services, and their
"rank will not affected when they rise in the re-
"gular course of succession.

"The Company owe so much to the eminent
"services of Major Popham, that I may think it
"incumbent upon me at a future period, to re-
"commend him to their further consideration.
"Whilst I bestow the just tribute of praise due
"to those officers who acted upon the spot, I
"should be guilty of an unpardonable neglect
"and even injustice, if I omitted to express my
"sense of equal approbation of the conduct of
"others more remote.

"Colonel Morgan on the first intelligence
"which reached him of my situation, and with-
"out waiting for official information or authority,
"in the true spirit of an able and zealous officer,
"detached a very considerable portion of his
"brigade, and all the supplies of provisions
"which he could procure.

"Sir

" Sir John Cumming likewise moved with the " utmost diligence and alacrity on receiving an " order to occupy the station of Cawnpoor, in " the room of the second brigade. He marched " with his whole force in fifteen hours after re- " ceiving the orders, and reached Cawnpoor in " four days, himself, officers, and troops, chear- " fully making their utmost efforts in the common " cause.

" Such have been the spirited and judicious " exertions of our officers and troops in support " of the Company's most valuable rights and " possessions, of the dignity of their government, " and of the honour and safety of their chief " magistrate; a conduct which manifests the " strongest attachment and affection on their parts, " and implies an observance of justice and regard " to the prosperity and happiness of those who " are placed under our authority, on ours. " These are circumstances which will always af- " ford me the most pleasing reflections, notwith- " standing the calamities which have produced " them.

" I have the honour to be, &c.

(Signed) " WARREN HASTINGS."

Chunar, 1st December, 1781.

 TRANS-

TRANSLATION of the Sunnud granted to Rajah Cheit Sing, for the Zemidarry of Gauzipore, Benares, &c.

Be it known to the Mutsedies in office, present and to come, Cannoongoes Muchudums, Ryatts, cultivators, to all the inhabitants and people resident and belonging to Sircar Benares, Gazypore, and Chundara, in the soubah of Illahabad, That wheareas by virtue of a treaty with the Nabob Assoph ul Dowlah, concluded on the 20th Rubby ul Owal, 1189, Hegeree, or 21st May, 1775, the Government and Sovereignty of the Sircars abovementioned, has been ceded to the Honourable East-India Company, from the 4th of Jummaddy ul Owal 1189 Hejeree, or 4th July, 1775, the said East-India Company therefore, in virtue of the rights thereby obtained, do confirm unto Rajah Cheit Sing, the Zemidarry, Aumeeny, and Poujedarry of the said Sircars agreeably to the Zemmell, together with the Cutwallus of Juanpore and Benares, and the Mint of Benares, from the said date. Whatever gold and silver shall be coined in the Mint, the said Rajah shall coin conformably to his Mutchulka. He is not to be, in the smallest particular, remiss in the observation and execution of the several duties incumbent on him he is to behave with moderation and kindness to the Ryatts and people, to promote the

cultivation

cultivation and encreafe of inhabitants and produce of the lands; expelling thieves, nightly affaulters and robbers, and fo effectually punifhing the difturbers of the peace, that no trace of them may be feen; and he is to pay a tribute of 23,40,249 Benares mutchuldar rupees, or 2266180 Calcutta ficcas, annually to the Company's Treafury; fhould he receive orders to pay the above revenue at Benares, he fhall, in that cafe, pay the fum of 23,40,249 Benares mutchuldar rupees, each rupee to weigh ten mafha, and to contain two ruttee and two chowls of alloy, and no more; fhould the weight be lefs, or the alloy be more, he fhall make up the deficiency; whenever the money fhall not be wanted at Benares, he is to remit the annual amount of 2366180 of ficca rupees punctually agreeable to his Kifts, and by monthly payments at Calcutta. In confideration of which, he fhall be allowed a deduction of two per cent. amounting in all to ficca repees 44,4,34 14 5 account of Hindownny or Exchange, which being deducted, the net amount is 22,21,745 17 ficca rupees of Calcutta, which he is to pay at that place. After the fettlement of accounts, at the end of the year, he fhall, in the cuftomary manner, receive credit for his payments, and he is by no means to collect the prohibited abwab of the durgah of his Majefty. This Sunnud being granted, is to remaid in force, and

and all former sunnuds to become null and void; you the Mutseddies and persons abovementioned, are to regard the said Rajah, as truly and lawfully possessed of the Zemidarry, Aumuny, and Poujedarry, of the above Sircars, and to acknowledge his authority in the several acts appertaining thereunto. Know that we have issued the most strict and positive commands, and obey them accordingly.

Written on the 25th of Suffer, 17th Sun, or 15th of April, 1776.

(Signed) By the Governor-General and Council.

The Zimmeen.

The office of the Zemindarry of Sircar Benares, Gazypore, Chundara, the Cuttwally, the duties and the mint in the Sobah of Illahabad, have been conferred upon the great Chief Rajah Cheit Sing Behadre, also the Aumuny and Poujedarry.

Copy of a Pottah granted to Chiet Sing.

The Pottah containing the underwritten stipulations is granted unto Rajah Chiet Sing Bahadre.

Sircar Benares, Gazeypore, Chunar, and the mahals of Sircar of Juanpore, comprehending the

maha

mahal and duties, Havily, Mahomed, Abaub, Benares, the Khaus Daums in Purgunna Bhadurry, Talook of Sunkeramow in Purgunna Chunar, Suklesgurra, Bijcepore, Sircar Gauzypore Purgunnah Sekunderpore Khered Shady Abaud Patna Serreinga, including the Cutwally duties of Juanpore and Benares, the mint of Benares, the mokumy, yatisaub and stores, weighing both maul and duties, and the Duanny, Dustore, excepting the narcar of half the Jagheer of Bhadurry, the exempted Jagheers of Ayma which have been inserted for a length of time in the accounts as deductions, all the articles of the Taheed are settled upon you from the 4th of Jumaudy ul Awaul 1189, Hijeree, or the 4th of July, 1775, English, at a stipulation per annum of 2340249 Mahidar Benares rupees, not short of the weight of 10 mosha each, and not containing a greater portion of alloy than two rattees, and two beringe, agreeably to your Mutchulka and Cabuleat. This sum you will therefore pay, but should it not suit the convenience of the company to receive it at Benares, you are to pay it in Calcutta in sicca rupees of Calcutta, amounting in which specie to 22,66,180 sicca rupees, the amount of the Hindooawn or exchange, allowed you at the rate of 2 per cent. is rupees 44434:14,5, which being deducted, the net sum will be 22,21,745,1,15 sicca rupees of Calcutta. This you are to pay without

without the leaſt deduction or depreciation whatever, in the courſe of each year by monthly payments, agreeably to your ſeparate keſtbundy. This you are to pay without any allowance for ſubundy, you will remit the money to Calcutta without fail, conformably to the ſaid kiſtbundy.

Kubboolyat, or agreement executed by Rajah Cheit Sing, for the Zemidarry of Benares, &c.

Whereas a treaty has been concluded between the Engliſh Eaſt India Company, and the Nabob Aſſoph ul Dowlah Chea Cawn Behadur, Huzzubber Jung Nazim of the Soubah of Allahabad, under date the 20th of Rubbee ul Awal 1189, Hijeree, or the 21ſt of May, 1775, Chriſtian, whereby the ſovereignty of the Sircars, Benares, Gauzeypore, Chunar, &c. hath been ceded to the Engliſh Eaſt India Company from the 4th of Jamady ul Awal 1189, Hijeree, or the 4th of July 1775, Chriſtian, and the Company having granted the Zemidarry, the Aumuny and Toujedarry of the aforeſaid Sircars, together with the Cutwallies of Benares and Juanpore, &c. and the mint of Benares unto me from the above date, I do hereby voluntarily conſent and agree under my hand, that whatever coins ſhall be ſtruck in the ſaid mint, ſhall be conformably to a ſeparate obligation, which I have executed under date the

25th

25th of Zihiza, in the 17th year of the reign, and delivered to the Government for the Company. It ſhall be my duty to do every thing that may be needful and uſual for the intereſt and ſecurity of the country, to provide for the welfare of the inhabitants—to be attentive to the encreaſe of cultivation and improvement of the revenue, to uſe my endeavours in ſuch manner to expel robbers and aſſaſſins, and to puniſh offenders of every kind, that not a trace of them may be left, and will pay the annual revenue of Government, being at Benares, mutchuldar rupees of Benares 2340249, each rupee to weigh no leſs than ten maſſa, and to contain no more alloy than two ruttas and two chowl, any deficiency of the ſtandard to be made good. If the Government ſhall not have occaſion to receive the ſame at Benares, I will, in ſuch caſe, pay it at Calcutta annually, by monthly payments, according to Kiſtbundy, and conformably to the Tuzul Zill, or particulars in the margin, the ſum being Calcutta ſicca rupees 22,66,180, including Nuzzeranna, &c. but deducting on account of Hoondyan, or exchange, a premium of two per cent. which premium of two per cent. upon the whole ſum, being ſicca rupees 44434,14,5, I will accordingly deduct from remitting the remainder to the Company's Treaſury at Calcutta, ſo that, after the deduction of Exchange, I ſhall pay net, and with-

 out

out further deduction into the Treasury of Calcutta, the sum of Calcutta sicca rupees 22,21,745115 at the end of each year. After payment of the same, and observing the conditions agreed upon, I shall receive a release or discharge in full, wherefore I have written the agreement to be adhered to accordingly.

In the margin follows a list, dated 25th Suffer, 17th of the monthly instalments Sun, corresponding with the 15th April, 1776, Christain.

Signed by the Rajah. | Seal of the Rajah. |

A true Copy, (Signed) E. HAY,

Sub-Secretary to the Hon. the Governor and Council.

Extract from the Secret Proceedings of the Hon. the Governor-General and Council, on the 9th July, 1778.

Resolved—That Rajah Cheit Sing be required in form, to contribute his share of the burthen of the present war, by the establishment of three regular battalions of sepoys, to be raised and maintained at his expence, and the Governor-general is requested to write to him to that effect.

Copy

Copy of a letter from Rajah Cheit Sing, received the 30th July, 1778.

I have been honoured by the receipt of your gracious letter, communicating the intelligence of a war being broke out between the Courts of Great Britain and France, and desiring me to take on myself a share of the burden of expence —my patron I am the servant of the Sircar—I will write you more fully hereafter—on all occasions I am hopeful of your Highness's favour and support.

Extract from the secret proceedings of the Honourable Governor-General and Council, on the 26th August, 1779.

Resolved, That the Commander in Chief be requested to give orders to Major Camac, or the officer in command of his detachment for the march of two battalions of sepoys to Benares, at the requisition of Mr. Thomas Graham, the resident there, and to remain at that place for further orders.

Resolved, that the following letter be written to Mr. Graham:

To Mr. Thomas Graham, President at Benares.

Sir,

We have received your letters of the 16th instant, acquainting us that Rajah Cheit Sing had declined to pay the five lacks of rupees which we required of him, as his proportion of the expences of the war for the present year.

Having judged it necessary to make this claim, which was suggested to us by the urgency of the case, we cannot admit of any plea which the Rajah may urge to exempt him from it; orders have therefore been sent to Major Camac, or the officer in command of his detachment, to march to Benares, immediately on your requisition, with two battalions of sepoys, and to wait our further orders at that place. We have thought this step necessary, for the purpose of compelling the Rajah to pay the quota required of him in case of necessity; and we desire that you repeat your demand, and insist on his compliance. If the Rajah still continue to object to your claim and refuse payment, you are to require the officer in in command of the detachment, to march immediately in conformity to your orders, and advise us of your proceedings. We hope, however, that you will not be reduced to proceed to this extremity, as it would oblige us to encreafe our demands on the Rajah, by exacting from him the whole expence of the detachment, from the day of its march, in addition to our original claim.

We are, &c.

Copy of a letter from Rajah Cheit Sing, received the 27th Auguft, 1779.

I have been honoured with your letter, calling on me for the payment of five lacks of rupees, on account of the expence of the war for the prefent year, and underftand its contents.

My fituation is well known to you, and I affure you, without referve, that I have no ability left, nor is there any mode of relief for me but in your favour.—I am fully confident that it is your defire, who are my mafter, to fupport me your fervant; and laft year you directed Shick Ally Nucky, that I fhould by any means, by difpofing of my effects, or by borrowing, make this one payment, and I fhould not be called on

in

in future, and that you would take very means for my advantage and suppport.

I accordingly put in practice every method in my power, and by loans made good the requisition. It is now absolutely out of my power to raise the sum required, and I am therefore hopeful that you will be kindly pleased to excuse me the five lacks now demanded, and that nothing may be demanded of me beyond the amount expressed in the Pottah, which through your favour I obtained from the honourable English Company.

This Raja and Zemidarry, and my dignity, are the gifts of your Highness. I have judged it necessary to represent to you my inability and helpless state.

Copy of a letter from Raja Cheit Sing, received 21st August, 1780.

I have been honoured by your orders, directing me to pay five lacks of Sicca Machuldar rupees to Mr. Fowke, of the war which still continues; and although my distressed situation must be known to you from other quarters, notwithstanding I have been afraid to represent it to you myself, that I have sold my house and borrowed sums

ſums of money, from which I am not yet releaſed; yet, in obedience to your orders, I have paid one lack of rupees out of the five lacks, to Mr. Fowke, and ſhould pay the other four in three months. I requeſt you will ſend directions to that gentleman to allow me that time, and it ſhall be punctually paid at the end of that term; you yourſelf muſt be convinced, that I have no abilities or reſources left.

Extract from the public proceedings from the 26th of October, 1780.

Copy of a letter to General Giles Stibbert, Commander in Chief, &c.

Having had late occaſion to be much diſſatisfied with the conduct of the Rajah of Benares towards this government, in withholding the payment of the amount due from him, as his ſubſidy: we think it neceſſary to direct and do direct you to iſſue orders to the commanding officers of the battalions at the ſtations neareſt to Benares, to march immediately to that place, and wait ſuch further orders as may hereafter be tranſmitted to them.

We are, &c.

Extract

Extract from the secret proceedings of the Honourable Governor-General and Council, on the 2d of November, 1780.

Agreed, That the Governor-General be requested to write to the Nabob Vizier, recommending to him to require from Fyzoola Cawn, the quota of troops stipulated by treaty, to be furnished by the latter for his service, being 5000 horse, to be put under the immediate command of Lieutenant-Colonel Muir, commanding at Futtighur.

Agreed also that the Governor-General be requested to write to the Rajah of Benares, requiring him to furnish such part of the cavalry entertained in his service, as he can spare for the service of this government, and to inform him what number he can supply; that a letter be written to Mr. Francis Fowke, directing him to make the same requisition of the Rajah, and at the same time to obviate any jealousy which the Rajah may conceive; that this may be converted to a permanent imposition upon him, by assuring him that the board will require the services of these forces no longer than while the present war lasts, after which they will be returned.

N. B. The Appendix to the Narrative contains, amongst other papers of great importance, the depositions of several Gentlemen in the Company's Service, and of many very respectable natives of Indostan, which will be printed entire in the Appendix hereafter. For the present, however, I have abbreviated many of them, as they will tend to prove to every impartial reader, that the rebellion of Cheit Sing was premeditated—Mr. Hastings's journey to Benares accelerated the revolt of the Rajah.

Affidavit of Major Eaton, commanding at Buxar.

Letter from Major Eaton to Thomas Graham, Esq. Resident at Benares, dated the 23d of May, 1779, complaining of the disaffected conduct of Rajah Cheit Sing and his officers, and of enormities committed by the latter.

Letter from Major Eaton to Francis Fowke, Esq. Resident at Benares, upon the same subject, dated 3d of November, 1780.

Mr. Fowke's answer to Major Eaton, expressing that he had no hope of obtaining redress, dated 8th November, 1780.

Letter from Major Eaton to Francis Fowke, Esq. dated 17th of November, 1780, representing the assault made by the Zemidar of Beerpoor on Ensign Basset, and the general enormities of the Zemidars of the jurisdiction of Rajah Cheit Sing.

Letters from Major Eaton to the Supreme Council, on the same subject.

Major Palmer's affidavit of the declared intentions of the Governor-General towards Cheit Sing.

Attestation of David Anderson, Esq. to the same effect.

Affidavit of Moonshy Gore Persaud—His imprisonment and sufferings—Ladders made for the attack of the Governor-General's quarters.

Affidavit of Hurryram Pundit—Forces which attended Cheit Sing to Buxar.

Affidavit of Moonshy Patnimul—Proclamation at Benares against protection of English gentlemen, on pain of death, and forfeiture of property.

Affidavit of Moonshy Gore Persaud, the same in substance as the foregoing.

Affidavit

Affidavit of Doond Sing, commandant—Attempts of the Rajah's brother to ſeduce him from the Company's ſervice in February, 1781.

Various affidavits of the inſurrections in Gorookpoor.

Solemn declaration of Ranny Golaub Koower, widow of Bulwant Sing—Preparations made at Ramnagur for attacking the Governor-General in his quarters—Diſaffection of Cheit Sing.

Affidavit of Gudrauge Sing, Killidar of Ramnagur—Murder of Mr. Hooker—Deſign to attack the Governor-General's quarters.

Affidavit of Hunder Sing, adjutant at Buxar—Attempts of the Rajah's brother to ſeduce the ſepoys of the garriſon—Inſolence of the Zemidar Force attendant on the Rajah at Buxar—Orders to reduce the fort of Buxar—Aſſault made on Enſign Baſſet, and other gentlemen, at Beerpoor.

Affidavit of Sheck Mahmud, commandant in Cheit Sing's ſervice—Liſt of forces which attended the Rajah to Buxar—Maſſacre at Shewalla—Deſigns to attack the Governor-General's quarters at Benares—Liſt of forces in the ſervice of Rajah Cheit Sing.

Various affidavits of the maſſacre at Shewalla.

Perwannah from Rajah Cheit Sing to Dadjoo Sing, to join him and cut off the Engliſh.

To ditto to join Futteh Shaw.

Affidavits of Nathaniel Middleton, Eſq.—Reports of Perwannah's iſſued by Cheit Sing, commanding the deſtruction of the Engliſh, and letters to the Nabob's Zemidars inciting them to rebel—Fidelity and attachment of the Nabob Vizier—Murders at Goſſel Gunge—The Miniſters of the Vizier's Mother encourage the diſaffection, and aſſiſt the levying of troops at Fyzabad for Cheit Sing.

Affidavit of Lieutenant Colonel Hannay, commanding a corps of ſepoys in the Nabob Vizier's ſervice—Hoſtile practices of the Begums at Fyzabad—Troops levied there publicly for Cheit Sing, with the encouragement of the eunuchs of both the Begums—Actual departure of 1000 levies—Remonſtrance made to the Bow Begum by the deponent without effect—Attack of Captain Gordon by Shumſhur Cawn, the Begum's Aumil—General diſaffection of Gorookpoor and all the country lying South of Fyzabad, fomented by the

Agents

Agents of Cheit Sing, and by the money furnifhed by him.

Affidavit of Major John Macdonald, commanding a battalion of fepoys in the Vizier's fervice—Infurrections of Gorookpoor excited by Cheit Sing, and encouraged by the Begums at Fyzabad—The rebellion of Cheit Sing preconcerted.

Affidavit of Captain David Williams, commanding a battalion of fepoys in the Vizier's fervice—Infurrections of Gorookpoor, and mutiny of his own fepoys.

Affidavit of Captain John Gordon, commanding a corps of fepoys in the Nabob Vizier's fervice—Hoftile acts of Shumfhire Cawn, Aumil of the Vizier's mother, attributed to the Begum.

Second affidavit of Lieut. Colonel Hannay—Plan concerted by the Begums to detain him at Fyzabad, and to feduce from him his followers.

Affidavit of Juan Henere Moordelai, private of the company of Chaffeurs, relating the circumftances of the maffacre of his comrades at Lutteefpoor.

To

To the Honourable WARREN HASTINGS,
Governor-General, &c. &c. &c.

SIR,

When I had laſt the honour of ſeeing you, I more than once urged my reaſons for thinking, that the rebellion of Rajah Cheit Sing was but a part of a larger and more extenſive plan, which was by good fortune of your arrival prematurely brought forward before all the parties to it were united and properly prepared for action. In ſupport of this belief, and to prove that I am far from being ſingle in the eſpouſal of it, I beg leave to trouble you with ſome extracts from the letters I received from Colonel Hannay, written from the time of the firſt breaking out of the rebellion to my return to Lucknow. His ſituation for obtaining the knowledge he imparts, his experience, and his judgment to guide what he advances, muſt make his ſentiments of weight and authority.

In his letter of the 8th of September, from Fayzabad, ſcarcely ten days after he had ſet about obeying the Nabob Vizier's orders to march with his force to your aſſiſtance, he writes "that the "whole country on the Eaſt ſide of the Gogra "was in arms and rebellion. His own troops "deſerting, and the ſingle companies ſcarce able

"to

" to join other detachments: the forts of Gurruckpore, Bilma, and Dumreagunge taken from the Aumils by the Zemidars; and that even Hircurrackes cannot paſs; ſo that all communication of intelligence from his other detachments, under Major M'Donald, Captain Williams, and Lieutenant Gordon, was cut off and at an end." He adds, "This town (Fayzabad) has more the appearance of belonging to Cheit Sing than the Vizier. The Begums have placed guards to prevent any of my people going to the Buzar in it.—Within theſe four days Shaak Chaan, with near one thouſand horſe and foot, has marched from hence to Benares (they were raiſed here) and I muſt confeſs, that for my own part, I have no doubt but Juwâr Ally Cawn, and Behar Ally Khan, through their agents, have ſtirred up all the diſturbances which extend from hence to Powey and Azimgur.—I have ſent Hoolaſs Roy to the Begum to enquire into the reaſon of my people being prevented from going into the town, Cheit Sing's being ſuffered to raiſe troops here, and why her ſervants attempted to prevent my getting boats to tranſport the Company's guns and horſe from Amora; I have alſo deſired ſhe will give orders for ſeizing the family of Shaak Chaan (abovementioned) and when Hoolaſs Roy returns, I will write you her anſwer. In

" Khyrabad

" Kyrabad Sylack, and all the country on the West " of the Gogra, between Fyzabad and Kyrabad, " the Aumils are flying before the Gongwars, and " cannon firing at all hours. Cheit Sing has sent " money to Futty Shaw, Ghinoo Roy, Ajectmull, " Zalim Sing, and all the refractory Rajahs, to " enable them to raise men. I this moment re- " ceived Gordon's account of the loss of his de- " tachment, which puts my march to join you " out of the question. It happened by the vil- " lainy of the Fouzdar of Tanda Shumsheer " Khan, a Cheelah of Bahar Ally Khan, who " turned his guns upon the detachment, and an " unfordable nullah in front and many thousands " of rajepoots, who had fought them all the way " from Chowra Ghaut, made the sepoys despair. " Zalim Sing, and Putty Puul Sing mean to at- " tack McDonald to-morrow, with two thousand " one hundred men. Behar Ally Khan deserves " death; as the loss of Gordon's detachment can " only be imputed to him—his Cheelah would " never have acted so damning a part without " orders from him. Jewâr Ally Khan, in the " Choke of Fyzabad, asks every man who bears " the appearance of a soldier, why he goes not to " Cheit Sing for service—I mention these circum- " stances that you may mention them to Mr. " Hastings and the Nabob, and the necessary

" steps

" steps be immediately taken, to prevent what " delay will render a very serious matter. A few " days more will lead the ferment which is here " to Lucknow. If the Nabob insists upon my " proceeding, I must bring every body with me, " for whoever is left behind will be sacrificed."

On the 7th September, Capt. Williams writes, " Upon my arrival here, I found that part of " Futty Shaw's, Ghunoo Roy's, and Ajectmull's " people had crossed to Manjowlay. They have " been urged to this step by Cheit, who has sup- " plied them with a considerable sum of money, " and promised them great sums, if they will put " the whole country into confusion—five thou- " sand men are on the opposite side of the river, " ready to cross. Futty Shaw has written to all " his adherents to be in arms. *Saudit Ally and* " *the Begums* are concerned deeply in the late " business." In a subsequent letter, received immediately after the above, but without date, Colonel Hannay says, " I have before told you " how violently the Begum's people inflame the " present disturbance; and, in addition to this, " the principal Zemidars and Rajahs have all " certificates under the seal of Cheit Sing, that he " will supply them with whatever money they " may require for subsisting all the troops they " can raise. In a very short time, I apprehend

" the greateſt part of the Nabob's dominions will
" be in the ſtate we are in here; *and it is the*
" *general belief of every man in this part of the coun-*
" *try, that the conduct I have related, is a concerted*
" *plan for the extirpation of the Engliſh.* What
" may be the ſituation of the reſt of the Nabob's
" dominions I know not; but it is moſt certain,
" that from Gooda to Manjee, and from Fyzabad
" to the Benares diſtrict, and acroſs from the
" Gogra to the Ganges, the country is in the ut-
" moſt ferment. Should the preſent diſturbances
" proceed from a plan of policy, it will be con-
" cealed from you as much as poſſible, and there-
" fore I take all poſſible means of communicating
" to you what I really know to be fact—I know
" not whether the Dawks paſs freely from you to
" Lucknow; but, if they do not, and no meaſure
" is immediately taken to bring about order, and
" draw the troops together, we may be deprived
" of all poſſible means of aſſiſting one another,
" and the army loſt by detached regiments: we
" have no communication with Bengal, and the
" troops on this ſide Benares are at preſent too
" much ſeparated to yield one another timely
" aſſiſtance. I hope to God a ſufficient force is
" ordered for the reduction of Cheit Sing, *for*
" *the people who are daily ſent to him, horſe and foot,*
" *from Fyzabad*, and the ſeat of rebellion I have
" before named is *very great*."

In

In his next of the 13th, he ſays, " That it is " impoſſible, in the general inſurrection which " now reigns almoſt univerſally, impoſſible for " me to get the force together the Nabob de- " manded, or to force my way to you with a " leſs. The greateſt anarchy prevails—the pre- " ſent inſurrection is ſaid, and believed to be, " with an intention to expel the Engliſh. I am " compelled to give up all the country below " Goonda—be upon your guard againſt the " Vizier, for there are many circumſtances to " make me believe he means to eſpouſe the " cauſe of Cheit Sing; the *Begums* have *almoſt* " *themſelves* recruited for him." In his next letter of the 18th he ſays, " If you meet with a check " at Benares, every man in the country is ready " to fall upon your ſcattered parties." " The ſtate " of the Vizier's dominions is in general beyond " deſcription! The inſurrection is not partial, " but generally ſpread throughout the whole, tho' " it rages moſt violently in the Mahls of Sultan- " pore, the Mahls from Fyzabad to the Benares " country, the Mahls on this laſt ſide of the Go- " gra and in Koonry, Khyrabad, and Syluck; and " if I may truſt to the information I have receiv- " ed, it is already begun, and will ſoon rage as " violently in the Shajehanpone, Rohilcund, Kora, " and the Doaub. I have already and repeatedly " informed you of the diſpoſitions of thoſe in

" Fyzabad, whichhas in fact been one of the great " sources of the insurrection, and the place of all " others in the Vizier's dominions which has supplied Cheit Sing with the greatest number of " troops. The old Begum does, in the most open " and violent manner, support Cheit Sing's rebellion and the insurrection; and the Nabob's mother's accursed eunuchs, are not less industrious " than those of the Burra Begum. Capital examples made of Jewar Ally Khan, and Behur " Ally Khan, would, I am persuaded, have the " very best effect." On the 20th, he says, after restating his own imminent danger, " I have already " written you so fully my reasons of being convicted of the treachery practised at Fyzabad, " and which I am afraid extends to your camp, " that I need to say no more on the subject, and " again mentions the general insurrections." The truth of these positions I found most fully proved upon my return, and observed, in particular, that the most vigorous efforts were limited to the Jageerdars, among whom the Begums, Fyzullah Khan, and Lutterfut Ally Khan, distinguished themselves. However, the Nabob's return, the victories gained by the troops with you in the total reduction of Cheit Sing's country, and the march of the two regiments from Cawnpore to our assistance here, have unitedly contributed to restore matters nearly to their usual tran-

tranquility. The example moſt neceſſary to be made of the two active and turbulent Eunuchs, mentioned by Colonel Hannay, remains yet to be done, as well as of a villain now in confinement, who had aſſembled 5000 Gongwars for the avowed purpoſe of reſcuing two principal ſtate priſoners from their confinement with the Nabob; and it is univerſally believed to make an attempt upon the Treaſury, for which he had fixed the day of the Duſſarah, but was moſt happily detected, ſeized only a day before by the vigilance of the Cutwal, and the fact proved by papers found in his houſe; unleſs ſpirits of this ſort be controuled, the worſt of conſequences may be expected from the negelct, ſhould, which God avert, any freſh opportunities occur.

I have the honour to be, with reſpect, Sir,

Your moſt obedient

Humble ſervant,

(Copy) NATH. MIDDLETON.

A true copy, ſigned E. Hay, Sub-Secretary to the Honourable Governor-General and Council.

Lucknow, the 17th October, 1781.

Minute

Minute of Meſſ. WHELER and MACPHERSON.

The Board having already paſſed their opinion in terms of the fulleſt approbation upon the Governor-General's conduct, and management, in the ſuppreſſion of the rebellion of Cheit Sing, and the regulation of the Province and City of Benares, they think it unneceſſary to repeat their opinion of thoſe meaſures.

They cannot, at the ſame time, but remark that the explanations which the Governor-General has given in ſome parts of his proceedings, during his firſt diſcuſſions with Cheit Sing, and ſubſequent to the convulſion, are rather an open avowal of the motives that actuated his mind, than the guarded repreſentations of a public officer, ſtating to his employers the meaſures which an extraordinary ſituation influenced, dictated, and juſtified.

To a liberal and candid tribunal, ſuch was the natural and certainly the wiſeſt appeal. The generoſity and juſtice of a Britiſh tribunal looks more to the real motives and zeal of their agent, than to the preconcerted artifice of his conduct, or the legal diſcriminations of his defence. Even where a public meaſure is unſucceſsful, the re-

ſponſibility

ſponſibility riſqued by the agent, if riſqued upon public principles, is frequently his juſtification, and, in many caſes, entitles him to applauſe.

In theſe diſtant dominions, if the ruling ſervants of the State attend more to thoſe rules and forms which protect from reſponſibility, than to an ardent purſuit of the public intereſt under every private riſque, the hands of adminiſtration may ſecure themſelves againſt condemnation, even though the country ſhould be loſt through their miſmanagement.

It was not by avoiding perſonal reſponſibility, that the ſervants of the public eſtabliſhed the Britiſh influence in Aſia, nor is it by ſuch cold precautions that our power is to be maintained, eſpecially at an hour of general hoſtility againſt us. The Board are led into theſe obſervations, from an ingenuous conſideration of the difficulties in which the Governor-General found himſelf involved at Benares, and a conviction of the motives under which he acted. The firſt were ſurmounted with ability and fortitude; the latter they moſt ſincerely believe do him real honour. Eaſy would be the taſk to approve the ſuppreſſion of the rebellion, and to ſtand diſconnected with any reſponſibility, by juſtifying thoſe acts which certainly precipitated the ſtorm from the cloud in which it had gathered.

Acts,

Acts, which judges at a distance, judges unoppressed with the natural embarrassments of this government, may with great speciousness of argument condemn. But the Board wish not, they cannot permit themselves to proceed so disingenuously or guardedly. They are at the same time aware that in a rigid investigation of the whole of this business, the following questions will be asked:

1st. Where were the Governor-General's particular instructions for such extraordinary demands upon Cheit Sing?

2d. Why was that Chief put in arrest, when he offered to make every concession?

3dly. Whether there was not a compact between him and the Company which specified that he was only to pay them a certain annual tribute?

Subsequent to the massacre of our troops, and the events that followed, no questions will be asked.—In answer to the first question, the Board think the Governor-General was fully authorized by the general tenor of his instructions.

The Governor-General having a deciding vote, could have written out and approved more particular

ticular inſtructions. There was a delicacy in the mode he preferred, and it compoſed a greater reſponſibility.

In regard to the ſecond queſtion, it is evident from Cheit Sing's anſwers, and preparations, and the whole tenor of his conduct before, and at the time, that nothing but arreſt could have convinced him of the Governor-General's determination.

That the arreſt was not intended to proceed further than the payment of a proper fine to the Company, who ſtood in the place of his ſovereign and benefactor, is evinced by the Governor-General's Anſwer to Cheit Sing after his confinement.

Had a total revolution in the adminiſtration of the Zemidarry been intended, the arreſt muſt have been affected with more force and greater marks of ſeverity.

That the officers who went to execute this ſervice, were convinced that no meaſure of determined ſeverity was intended againſt Cheit Sing, appears from that unfortunate want of precaution which coſt them and their followers their lives.

In this conversation, which was private, the Rajah and Saadat Alli, were said to have talked of Hyder Ally's victory over Colonel Bailie's detachment, to have agreed, that they ought to seize this opportunity of consulting their own interests, and to have determined to watch the success of Hyder's arms. Some days after this conversation was said to have happened, I was informed by the same person, that the Rajah had received a message from one of the Begums at Fyzabad, (I think it was from Shujah ul Dowlah's widow) advising him not to comply with the demands of government, and encouraging him to expect support in case of his resisting. This also I believe I communicated to Mr. Markham; but not being perfectly certain, I now think it my duty to remove the possibility of your remaining unacquainted with a circumstance which may not be unconnected with the present conduct of the Rajah.

With great respect, Sir,

Your obliged and obedient servant,

(Signed) FRANCIS BALFOUR.

F I N I S.

Books printed for J. DEBRETT, (Succeſſor to Mr. ALMON.)

AN INQUIRY into the Manners, Taſte, and Amuſements of the two laſt Centuries in England, by John Andrews, LL. D. Price 2s. 6. ſewed.

The DEAN and the 'SQUIRE: a Political Eclogue, humbly dedicated to Soame Jenyns, Eſq. by the Author of the HEROIC EPISTLE to SIR WILLIAM CHAMBERS, &c. &c. a new edition, being the 4th, with additions. Price 1s. 6d.

An HEROIC EPISTLE to Sir WILLIAM CHAMBERS, Knt. the 14th edition. Price 1s.

An HEROIC POSTSCRIPT to the Public, occaſioned by their favourable reception of the HEROIC EPISTLE, 8th edition. Price 1s.

ODE to Mr. PINCHBECK, 5th edition. Price 6d.

An EPISTLE to Dr. SHEBBEARE Price 1s. 6d.

*** The above five are by the ſame author, and being all printed in 4to. may be had in boards, Price 6s.

An ANSWER to the DISQUISITION on GOVERNMENT and CIVIL LIBERTY, in a Letter to the Author of Diſquiſitions on ſeveral Subjects. Price 1s.

BLAKE'S REMARKS on COMMODORE JOHNSTONE'S account of his Engagement with Monſ. de Suffrein, a new edition, to which is prefixed a Letter from Blake to the Commodore, and a plan of the harbour. Price 1s.

The SPEECH of the Right Honourable CHARLES JAMES FOX, at a General Meeting of the Electors of Weſtminſter, aſſembled in Weſtminſter-Hall, July 17, 1782, in which are given the reaſons for withdrawing himſelf from the Cabinet; alſo an account of the whole of the proceedings on that day. Taken in ſhort hand by Mr. Blanchard, illuſtrated with an elegant and correct likeneſs of the Right Hon. Mr. Fox. Price 1s.

A SEAMAN'S REMARKS on the Britiſh Ships of the Line, from the 1ſt of January, 1756, to the 1ſt of January, 1782.—With ſome occaſional Obſervations on the Fleets of the Houſe of Bourbon. Price 6d.

Extract of an original Letter from Calcutta, relative to the Adminiſtration of Juſtice, by Sir Elijah Impey. Price 1s. 6d.

ORIGINAL MINUTES on the Appointment of Sir Elijah Impey to be Judge of the Sudder Dewanny Adawlett. Price 1s.

ORIGINAL MINUTES of the Governor General and Council of *Fort William* on the Settlement and Collection of the Revenues of Bengal: with a Plan of Settlement recommended to the Court of Directors, by PHILIP FRANCIS, ESQ. Price 7s. 6d. in boards.

General

B O O K S.

General Burgoyne's State of his Expedition from Canada, with all the authentic documents, and many circumstances not made public before. Written by himself. Illustrated with six plans of the action, the country, &c. finely engraved and coloured. A new edition, in 8vo. Price 6s. in boards.

Thoughts on Hunting, in a series of Letters, by Peter Beckford, Esq. a new edition, with an elegant frontispiece, by Bartolozzi. Price 7s. 6d. in boards.

Travelling Anecdotes through various parts of Europe, with plates, vol. 1, in boards. Price 6s.

On the Debt of the Nation, compared with its Revenue, and the impossibility of carrying on the War without Public Œconomy. Price 2s.

In the REMEMBRANCER, No. 88, is given an authentic copy of the answer of Major-General James Cuninghame to the charges exhibited against him by the House of Assembly to his Majesty, for his removal from the Government of the Island of Barbadoes. Price 1s.

In the PARLIAMENTARY REGISTER, No. 40 and 41, are given the whole of the very interesting correspondence between Lord Sackville, Sir Henry Clinton, and Earl Cornwallis, which Letters were laid on the table of the House of Lords, in consequence of the motion of His Grace the Duke of Chandos, with some anthentic Letters from Earl Cornwallis to Sir Henry Clinton, which were not produced to the House, and are the Letters which were alluded to in the course of the debate, as tending to throw an important light on the surrender of Earl Cornwallis.

Of whom may be had, the Parliamentary Register of the first Session of the Present Parliament, in 4 large vols. in 8vo. Price 1l. 11s. half bound and letter'd. The interesting Reports made by the Commissioners of the Public Accounts, with the Appendixes, containing the Examinations on Oath. Also the Reports of the Committees on East India Affairs; together with every important Paper laid upon the Table of either House of Parliament, are inserted in this Work.

An Essay on the Nature of a Loan, being an Introduction to the Knowledge of the Public Accounts. Price 6d.

The Earl of Abingdon's two late Speeches in the House of Lords, upon the Affairs of Ireland, with his Lordship's Celebrated Bill upon the same occasion. Price 6d.

An authentic List of both Minority and Majority, upon the motions made by Sir James Lowther against the American War, printed on a large sheet, in red and black. Price 2d. or 12s. per hundred,